THE TRUE MEANING OF
CHRISTMAS

THE TRUE MEANING OF
CHRISTMAS

The Birth of Jesus and the Origins of the Season

Michael Patrick Barber

Foreword by John C. Cavadini

IGNATIUS PRESS
San Francisco

AUGUSTINE INSTITUTE
Greenwood Village, CO

Cover art:
The Adoration of the Shepherds by Bartolomé Murillo, 1668/1669.
Cover design by Ben Dybas

© 2021 by Ignatius Press, San Francisco,
and the Augustine Institute, Greenwood Village, CO
All rights reserved.
Unless otherwise noted, biblical translations are the author's.
There may be some overlap with other English Bible translations.
Hardback ISBN: 978-1-950939-84-8
Paperback ISBN: 978-1-950939-85-5
Library of Congress Control Number 2021942440
e-Book ISBN: 978-1-955305-08-2
Audio ISBN: 978-1-955305-12-9
Printed in Canada ∞

To my parents, Patrick and Theresa Barber,
who first taught me the true meaning of Christmas

Contents

Foreword by John C. Cavadini   xi

1. **"I'll Be Home for Christmas": An Introduction**   1

   The Magic of Christmas   2

   The True Meaning of Christmas   3

   Christmas as "Christ's Mass"   4

   What Everyone Should Know about Christmas   6

2. **"O Come, O Come, Emmanuel": Ancient Jewish Hopes for a Messiah**   7

   Captive Israel   8

   Jewish Expectations for a Messiah   11

   Freedom from Sin   17

3. **"Tidings of Comfort and Joy": Gabriel's Announcement to Zechariah**   23

   Zechariah's Temple Service and Gabriel's Appearance   24

   The God Who Answers Prayers   27

   Prepare the Way of the Lord   30

4. **"Christ Is Born of Mary": Gabriel's Announcement to Mary**   37

   Christ the Lord   38

Full of Grace   43

The Lord Is with You   47

5. "Round Yon Virgin": Why a *Virgin* Mother   51

A Virgin Shall Conceive   51

Mary as Virgin   58

The New Creation   66

6. "What Child Is This?": Joseph and His Dilemma   71

The Royal Carpenter   72

Joseph the Carpenter   73

Joseph's Response to Mary's Pregnancy   75

Joseph's Example of Faith   80

7. "Away in a Manger": Jesus' Birth in Bethlehem   85

The Little Town of Bethlehem   86

The Manger Scene   88

The Manger and the Bread of Life   94

8. "Angels We Have Heard on High": The Shepherds
   in the Field   99

Why Shepherds?   100

Tidings of Comfort and Joy   101

Heaven's Army and Peace on Earth   104

9. "Star of Wonder": The Mysterious Magi   111

Who Are the Magi?   112

The Christmas Star 120

The Cradle and the Cross 125

10. "Christ Our God to Earth Descendeth":
The Historical Figure of Jesus 133

The Claims of Jesus Mythicists 134

Jesus in Historical Memory 136

The Gospels and History 140

11. "The First Nowell": How December 25 Became
Christmas 147

The Time of Jesus' Birth in the Gospel of Luke 149

Christmas and Paganism 152

Ancient Attempts to Date Jesus' Birth 156

The Winter Solstice 161

12. "It's Beginning to Look a Lot Like Christmas":
The Development of the Christmas Celebration 167

Christmas as a Season 168

Celebrating Christmas among the Ancient Pagans 171

The War on Christmas 174

How Saint Nicholas Became Santa Claus 180

Acknowledgments 189

Subject Index 191

Scripture Index 195

Foreword

By John C. Cavadini

Early in the third century, the brilliant catechist, exegete, and apologist Origen of Alexandria wrote one of the most beautiful passages bequeathed to us from patristic antiquity. Although the original Greek is lost, it still shines out in the Latin translation in which it was preserved. By this slender thread of witness, it has survived to the present day, to awaken anew in every age the ever-living wonder of the Incarnation.

Origen first invites the reader to contemplate the majesty of the divine nature of the Word of God. So great is this Word that he is called by Scripture "the image of the invisible God" (Colossians 1:15), and it is said that "in him were created all things visible and invisible, whether thrones or dominions or principalities or powers, all were created through him" (Colossians 1:16). His nature is "nothing else but the primal and ineffable nature of deity." And, as though this were going to conclude his contemplation, Origen continues, "For it is impossible to put into writing all that belongs to the Savior's glory."

But then, having ascended to the summit of contemplation of this glory, we find a new and unexpected vista revealed to

---

1   Origen, *On First Principles* 2.6.1, trans. G. W. Butterworth (repr., Notre Dame, IN: Ave Maria Press, 2013), 135, with slight adaptations. All translations of this work and biblical passages are taken from this edition.

2   Ibid., 2.6.2.

3   Ibid., 2.6.1.

our gaze: "When, therefore, we consider these great and marvelous truths about the nature of the Son of God, we are lost in the deepest amazement that such a being, towering high above all, should have 'emptied himself' (Philippians 2:7) of his majestic condition and become man and dwelt among men." No less than the Father himself bears witness (Matthew 3:17; Mark 1:11; Luke 3:22; cf. John 1:34), confirmed by miracles wrought by the Son and by the Spirit-inspired words of prophet and apostle alike, recorded in Scripture.

Origen continues,

> But of all the marvelous and splendid things about him, there is one that utterly transcends the limits of human wonder and is beyond the capacity of our weak mortal intelligence to think of or understand, namely, how this mighty power of the divine majesty, the very Word of the Father, and the very Wisdom of God, in which were "created all things visible and invisible" (Colossians 1:16), can be believed to have existed within the compass of that man who appeared in Judaea; yes, and how the wisdom of God can have entered into a woman's womb and been born as a little child and uttered noises like those of crying children; and further, how it was that he was troubled, as we are told, in the hour of death, as he himself confesses when he says, "My soul is sorrowful even unto death" (Matthew 26:38; Mark 14:34); and how at the last he was led to that death which is considered by men to be the most shameful of all,—even though on the third day he rose again.

Note that precisely what is featured in this passage, what is wonderful beyond wonder, is that he who already had a claim on our wonder because of his divine majesty, "emptied

---

4   Ibid., 2.6.2.

himself" (Philippians 2:7). That he would put aside such majesty is unimaginable—especially to a culture, such as that of Origen's time and, equally, of our own, fixated on status and rank, on prestige and celebrity. Nevertheless, he did! Even to the point of gestation in a woman's womb and birth as a child, crying as all little children do. How undignified! More undignified even than the humiliation of crucifixion, since at least such a death can be borne nobly, while there can be no noble bearing in an infant's wailing.

And yet that is the wonder of Christmas, the birth of a crying child from the womb of a mother into a life where suffering is invariably its destiny. Its wonder is, in a way, its very familiarity.

> What wondrous love is this, O my soul, O my soul?
> What wondrous love is this, O my soul?
> What wondrous love is this that caused the Lord of Bliss
> To bear the fearful curse for my soul, for my soul,
> To bear the fearful curse for my soul? ("What Wondrous
>   Love Is This")

The all-too-familiar familiarity of the human estate into which the Word is born marks the wondrous gift of self-emptying love that begs even our ability to wonder.

> When, therefore, we see in him some things so human that they appear in no way to differ from the common frailty of mortals, and some things so divine that they are appropriate to nothing else but the primal and ineffable nature of deity, the human understanding with its narrow limits is baffled, and struck with amazement at so mighty a wonder knows not which way to turn, what to hold or whither to betake itself.

---

5   Ibid.

Our understanding is "narrow" not only because it is finite but because it is "mortal," that is, hemmed in by the "curse" of our own state, so fragile, so subject to so much irreparable loss, or so it seems. We are afraid to love. We are afraid to love as the Word did, to empty ourselves into such loss. The very lavishness of the self-emptying love of the Word so challenges our narrow limits to proclaim it that "to utter these things in human ears and to explain them by words far exceeds the powers we possess either in our moral worth or in mind and speech."

But according to Origen, we're in good company, since to utter these things as they should be uttered "transcends the capacity even of the holy apostles; nay more, perhaps the explanation of this mystery lies beyond the reach of the whole creation of heavenly beings"! *O magnum mysterium!*

Barber reminds us that, of course, the "heavenly beings," the angels, do bear witness, precisely to the self-emptying of the Word, for they do not come to the rescue of this Prince of Peace, as Caesar's soldiers might come to the rescue of Caesar (see p. 105), but they sing of the *joy* (Luke 2:10) of so great a gift of love. Even the stars participate. The Lord's act of love exposes the lie of the devil, that there is no such thing as love, and so enables the magi to break out of the spell of astrology (see p. 115) and the stars to be released from their bondage to the devil's magic. They can recall, and proclaim with joy, this love which is the very same love in which they were created. They are free to be simply themselves and happily now guide the magi, and the reader of the Gospels alongside them, to the Savior's self-emptied glory, the glory in which the world was created and is now even becoming "a new creation" (see pp. 66–67).

---

6 Ibid.
7 Ibid.

Can this magnificent glory and the wonder it evokes possibly leverage its way into our narrowly closed hearts? Can we learn to "live in the shade of this mystery," where, as Origen mentions, "our life is hid with Christ in God" (Colossians 3:1)? Yes!—because the mystery of this breathtaking self-emptying love, though its conception is miraculous, comes with none of the fanfare of so mighty a miracle but is itself *hid with Christ* in the beguiling charm and intimate life of a family. The mystery of the Incarnation is thus the very mystery of Christmas.

Origen points especially to the role of Saint Joseph in keeping this mystery hidden. Joseph himself occupies a space of hiddenness; he is "easy to forget about" as "he quietly fades into the background" (see p. 71). His identity as a "royal carpenter" (see p. 72) shows us that he, too, is configured to the mystery of the divine self-emptying. Origen comments that it is because of Saint Joseph that the virginal conception and childbearing of the Savior by Mary are kept hidden from the evil one. The miracle is received into the intimacy of marriage and family, hidden there, welcomed there—not only by the "grace" of Mary but by the "righteous" Saint Joseph, whose solicitous protection and providing for a Son who is not naturally his own weaves a cloak of invisibility, of paternal love, around this whole family, an exhibition of "foolishness" that the devil cannot see through because he, who does not believe in love, expects any divine power worth its salt to be exhibited in a daunting and dazzling display. But the "foolishness of God is wiser than men, and the weakness of God is stronger than men" (1 Corinthians 1:25). The gaze of the

8   Ibid., 2.6.7.
9   Origen, *Homilies on the Gospel of Luke* 6.4. For these passages, see John C. Cavadini, "The Fatherly Heart of St. Joseph," *Church Life Journal,* January 26, 2001, https://churchlifejournal .nd.edu/articles/the-fatherly-heart-of-saint-joseph/.
10 See ibid., 6.5.

devil cannot see past the haze of love, of the sharing of hearts, tried by struggles and buoyed by prophecy, that is the life of this family. As the Christmas carol "O Little Town of Bethlehem" exclaims, "How silently, how silently the wondrous gift is given!"—heralded only by the angels and only in the dead silence of midnight.

Almost as silently does this little book, upon which the reader is about to embark, work to recover "the sacred page" of Scripture as the very "soul of sacred theology." Without any particular display to mark its erudition, its use of historical contextual considerations, honoring the human authorship of Scripture, deployed in the service of an interpretation of Scripture as an inspired whole, properly contextualized in its own pages and in the Tradition of the Church, honors equally its divine authorship.

Isn't this approach itself also a way of honoring the wonder of the Incarnation? For "indeed the words of God, expressed in human language, are in every way like human speech, just as the Word of the eternal Father, when he took on himself the weak flesh of human beings, became like them."

Scripture is itself a wonder of Incarnation, proclaiming the story of Jesus, which is not simply "a metaphor or a symbol," or, to put it bluntly, a myth (see p. 145), but rather a mystery, hidden without fanfare in the bosom of a poor family, and equally, humbly hidden in the hospitably human words of Sacred Scripture. Can we develop a truly biblical pedagogy of wonder, commensurate with the mystery hidden in the Bible? That is what Michael Patrick Barber offers us. So, as Origen writes, let us "pursue our contemplation with all fear and reverence ... in such a way that nothing unworthy or unfitting

---

11 Vatican Council II, Dogmatic Constitution on Divine Revelation *Dei Verbum* (November 18, 1965), no. 24.

12 Ibid., 11–12.

13 Ibid., 13.

may be thought to reside in that divine and ineffable existence, nor on the other hand may the events of his life be supposed to be the illusions caused by deceptive myths." For it is the glory of Scripture that "the divine character of Scripture is hidden under a poor and lowly style, 'a treasure in earthen vessels' (2 Corinthians 4:7)."

O magnum mysterium! "Christ our God to earth descendeth!" (see p. 133).

This Christmas, and for many to come, may this little book help such a mystery to be reborn into our own wondering hearts!

---

14 Origen, *On First Principles* 2.6.2.
15 Ibid., 4.1.7.

"I'll Be Home for Christmas":
An Introduction

But it's Christmas.

Those three little words are almost irrefutable. Behind them is an appeal to an unspoken assumption: at Christmas, we can expect more from one another. At this time of year, we strive to be better.

No one expressed the lofty aspirations people have for the season more eloquently than Charles Dickens. Near the beginning of his immortal tale *A Christmas Carol*, we find Fred explaining to his uncle Scrooge why Christmas is unique:

> [Christmas is] a kind, forgiving, charitable, pleasant time: the only time I know of, in the long calendar of the year, when men and women seem by one consent to open their shut-up hearts freely, and to think of people below them as if they really were fellow-passengers to the grave.

Scrooge, of course, will have none of it. His dismissive retort to those who so cherish the season is well known: "Bah! Humbug." Yet, as almost everybody knows, a series of encounters with memorable ghosts famously changes his mind. Moreover, it was not only Scrooge who was affected.

Dickens' novel has left an indelible mark on the way people think about Christmas. This is not to say that Christmas had not been observed before Dickens' time; it most certainly was. Later in this book, we will discuss the development of the Christmas celebration. For now, we can simply point out that by the late 300s the feast of Christ's birth was already becoming a major holy day for early Christians. It was called the "nativity," from the Latin, *nativitas*, which means "birth." In a homily delivered sometime between A.D. 386 and A.D. 388, the ancient Christian preacher John Chrysostom calls it "the chief and mother of all holy days."[1]

Yet even though Christians saw it as an important day, it has not always been viewed as the major holiday and cultural event it is recognized as today. As we shall see at the end of this book, in the 1600s Christmas was even outlawed for a time both in England and in certain American colonies. Surprisingly, it was not atheists who opposed it, but certain self-professed Christians. By Dickens' day, it was no longer illegal. Nonetheless, Dickens had an important role in transforming the day from an occasion of feasting to something more poignant.[2]

The Magic of Christmas

Today, Christmas is more than just another holiday. It is associated with our deepest longings. This is often expressed in Christmas music.

While some Christmas songs are just plain silly, many of the most memorable ones connect the day to matters closest to our hearts. Consider these familiar lines:

---

1   John Chrysostom, *Homilies VI against the Anomoeans* 6.23, trans. Paul W. Harkins, in *On the Incomprehensible Nature of God* (Washington, DC: Catholic University of America Press, 1984), 174.

2   See Timothy Larsen, "The Nineteenth Century," in *The Oxford Handbook of Christmas*, ed. Timothy Larsen (Oxford: Oxford University Press, 2020), 35–50.

I'll be home for Christmas
If only in my dreams. ("I'll Be Home For Christmas")

I'm dreaming of a White Christmas
Just like the ones I used to know. ("White Christmas")

Christmas is associated with *dreaming*—and dreaming about things that are especially dear to us. At Christmastime our thoughts turn to our loved ones and to the notion of going home.

Christmas is also associated with *magic*. No one, at least in my experience, speaks of Labor Day or New Year's Day as "magical." Christmas magic? Everyone has heard of *that*.

There is also a sense that Christmas is a time to be grateful for what we have in the present. As the lyrics to one song put it:

Here we are as in olden days
Happy golden days of yore
Faithful friends who are dear to us
Gather near to us once more. ("Have Yourself a Merry
    Little Christmas")

The line about gathering with our friends "once more" is poignant. We are unsure how many future gatherings there will be with them. Someday the present will become the "golden days of yore."

The True Meaning of Christmas

Our hopes for Christmas, however, are often set impossibly high. Given such expectations, it is not surprising that people often feel let down by the end of the season. There are many reasons for this. For one thing, we measure our experiences of the present by our recollections of the past. Since our memories are often idealized, the Christmas of today can easily seem to pale in comparison to those of yesteryear. In addition, our hopes for Christmas are often deflated by discovering that stories of the "magic" of Christmas were made up or greatly exaggerated. This can lead to a kind of cynicism. Many conclude that Christmas is not, in the end, what it is cracked up to be. Maybe there can be no going home.

Although there are some falsehoods about Christmas and its origins that I would like to set straight, my focus in this book is not primarily myth-busting. Instead, I will argue that Christmas can only be disappointing when its true meaning is forgotten. I will show that when we understand what Christmas is *really* about, we can never be let down by it. As we will see, Christmas involves an invitation to a homecoming that surpasses our deepest longings. The problem is most people do not know the Christmas story well enough. The purpose of key aspects of the Christmas celebration have often been forgotten.

Christmas as "Christ's Mass"

Let us return for a moment to Dickens' famous story about Scrooge. When Fred explains to his miserly uncle why Christmas is so special, he begins with a key statement. Before talking about Christmas as a kind and charitable season, Scrooge's nephew makes a vitally important observation. He says that "veneration" is to be given to Christmas "*because of its sacred name and origin*" (emphasis added). Dickens is subtle but his meaning is unmistakable. For Fred (and for Dickens), Christmas is sacred because, as its name reveals, it is about *Christ*.

For Dickens, this is the *first* reason Christmas is special. All the associations Fred makes with the season—its relationship to joy and good will—are anchored in the recognition that it is primarily about Jesus. This is why Fred does not simply say Christmas should be "celebrated"; for Fred, the day is to be "venerated."

Yet, as far as I can recall, I have never seen a television or movie version of Dickens' book that includes this dimension of Fred's explanation. This is profoundly troubling. By omitting this detail, retellings of Dickens' classic story hollow out his view of Christmas, reducing it to little more than a season of sentimentality.

There is another element of Dickens' story that is typically left out of adaptations of it. When Scrooge wakes up and discovers he has not missed Christmas, the now-converted man—who is introduced in the first chapter as a "covetous old sinner"—does something poignant. Before heading to Bob Cratchit's house with gifts for Tiny Tim and his family, he has another priority. When Scrooge leaves his home, Dickens says, "He went to church." I do not remember ever seeing a depiction of Scrooge's presence at a church service in movie versions of Dickens' tale.

The last line of *A Christmas Carol* announces that Scrooge "knew how to keep Christmas well." Dickens does not spell it out, but he surely knew that his audiences would connect going to church to observing Christmas rightly. For Dickens, going to church was an essential aspect of Christmas. *Just as there is no "Christmas" without Christ, there is also no Christmas without "Mass."* "Christmas" literally means "Christ's Mass." In the Church of England of Dickens' day, it was not unusual for church services to be called "Mass," a term many Anglicans still use today. For Dickens, Christmas would be incomplete apart from going to church. As we shall see, this is an idea that is deeply rooted in the Bible's portrayal of Jesus' birth.

What Everyone Should Know about Christmas

This book is for people who want to deepen their experience of the Christmas season. As I will show, to find our way "home" at Christmas, we first need to return to Christmas' home in the story of the Bible. Only by carefully reflecting on the stories of Jesus' birth there can we hope to celebrate Christmas in the way it is meant to be celebrated. Only then can we discover the real joy it promises.

The last chapters of this book also explore the development of Christmas. Among other things, we will see the following:

- How Christmas came to be celebrated on December 25
- Why there are "Twelve Days" of Christmas
- Saint Nicholas' transformation into Santa Claus
- The symbolism that gave rise to the use of Christmas trees

At virtually every turn we will see how Christmas brings us back to the lessons taught in the Bible.

Among other things, what we will discover is that the Christmas story emphasizes that God has sent us the Son to bring us into communion. The major players in the Gospel accounts of Jesus' birth—Zechariah, Elizabeth, Mary, Joseph, the shepherds, and the magi—are more than "characters." They are part of a family—the family of God—into which we are invited.

To begin our discussion, let us focus on the word at the heart of Christmas: *Christ*. Why is Jesus called by this name? What does it tell us about him, and why is it important to the celebration of Christmas today? To answer these questions, we need to go back and read the stories about Jesus in their original context, namely, the first-century Jewish world.

2

"O Come, O Come, Emmanuel": Ancient Jewish Hopes for a Messiah

It was a late night and I still had lots of driving ahead of me. I knew I needed to find a way to stay awake and alert. Listening to music was not helping, so I flipped on the car radio. I happened on a program that was discussing Christianity's impact on the world. It turned out to be just the thing I needed—but not for the reasons I had hoped.

The host explained that though he was not Christian, he wanted to discuss Christianity in a respectful way. Unfortunately, what he had to say exposed his profound ignorance of the faith. He repeatedly referred to Jesus as "Mr. Christ." It was infuriating—but, I also admit, pretty funny. Turning on the radio was the right move. I was now wide awake.

"Christ" was not Jesus' last name. Ancient Jews did not have last names. When Joseph and Mary went about town, they were not addressed as "Mr. and Mrs. Christ." So how did Jesus become Jesus *Christ*?

In this chapter, we will explore the meaning of the word "Christ"—that is, "Messiah"—by examining ancient Jewish expectations. For Jews of Jesus' day, the coming of a messiah represented nothing less than the realization of all of God's promises. Along the way, this chapter will explain the words of the well-known hymn "O Come, O Come, Emmanuel,"

7

whose English lyrics were translated by John Mason Neale in 1861:

> O come, O come, Emmanuel
> And ransom captive Israel
> That mourns in lonely exile here
> Until the Son of God appear.

What does "Emmanuel" mean? Why does Israel need to be "ransomed" from "exile"? As we will see, the song's words beautifully encapsulate key aspects of ancient Jewish hopes, which also reflect our own longings—our longing to escape from "exile" and return home.

Captive Israel

In Jesus' day, it seemed as if Rome had conquered the world. Romans referred to their domination as "peace," yet that was hardly the word Jews would have chosen. Led by General Pompey, Roman forces had invaded Jerusalem in 63 B.C. They desecrated the temple and asserted their rule over the land. While the situation looked bleak, those who knew the Scriptures understood two things. First, Jews believed that their enemies had triumphed over them for a reason. Second, they trusted that God had a plan to save them. Without understanding these things, we cannot properly interpret the accounts of Jesus' birth in the New Testament.

Lonely Exile

Just before his death in the book of Deuteronomy, Moses delivers a series of speeches to Israel. Here he provides a preview of what will happen to the people of Israel in the future. He tells them that if they keep God's commandments, they will thrive in the Promised Land and find safety from their enemies (Deuteronomy 28:1–14). Yet Moses also warns them that if they disobey God's law, they will trigger a series of divine punishments. We read:

> The LORD shall cause you to be defeated before your enemies.... The LORD will bring a nation against you from far away ... a stern-faced nation who shall not respect the old or show mercy to the young." (Deuteronomy 28:25, 49–51)

In the end, Moses declares that Israel will fall into sin. Their enemies will carry them off into exile: "the LORD will scatter you among all peoples, from one end of the earth to the other" (Deuteronomy 28:64).

Jews in Jesus' day understood that Moses had correctly prophesied the future. In the Scriptures, the history of Israel unfolds just as Moses predicted it would. After his death, the Israelites enter the Promised Land and ultimately obtain rest from their enemies under King David (2 Samuel 7:1). When his son, Solomon, comes to power, the twelve tribes of Israel live together in harmony and enjoy peace with the nations (1 Kings 4:20–21). After his death, however, the kingdom begins to disintegrate. Why does this happen? Because the people turn away from the God of their fathers and worship other gods.

The northern tribes of Israel end up being conquered by the nation of Assyria and are carried off as exiles in about 722 B.C. Later in 587 B.C., the Babylonians conquer Jerusalem and take the rest of the people off into exile as well. However, they do eventually return.

Babylon falls to Persia in about 539 B.C., and the Jews are given permission by the Persian king to go back to their land.

But when they return, they are continually persecuted by their enemies. This suffering is viewed as a kind of continuation of the exile (Ezra 9:8–9; Nehemiah 9:36). In Jesus' day, many Jews understood the Roman oppression of Judea as part of the exile experience. Their sins had led to captivity to pagan powers.

Still, all was not lost. Through the prophets, God announced that a day would come when they would be delivered. Israel and the former kingdom of David would one day be restored.

Prepare the Way of the Lord

In the book of Isaiah, we read about a glorious future in which God will console Israel:

> Comfort, comfort my people,
> says your God.
> Speak to the heart of Jerusalem,
> and cry to her that her service has ended.
> that her penalty is paid. . . .
> A voice cries out:
> "In the wilderness prepare the way of the LORD,
> make straight in the desert a highway for our God." (Isaiah
>   40:1–3)

The Lord's great love for Israel is on full display in these lines. First, we see that comfort is announced because the people's "penalty" will come to an end. Second, and more importantly, the prophet reveals that the deliverer of Israel will be none other than God. A "way"—a "road"—is being prepared in the wilderness. Who is coming on it? The *Lord.*

Going on, an important expression is used for the message of Israel's deliverance: "good tidings." The future day of Israel's redemption is linked with the following declaration:

> Get you up to a high mountain, O Zion, herald of *good tidings*; lift up your voice with strength, O Jerusalem, herald of *good tidings*, lift it up, fear not; say to the cities of Judah, *"Behold your God!"* (Isaiah 40:9)

In the ancient Greek translation of the Old Testament called the Septuagint, the word translated "good tidings" (Greek: *euangelizomenos*) is closely related to the term translated "Gospel" (Greek: *euangelion*) in the New Testament. The word used by Isaiah means to herald the good news—the gospel. What is this "good news"? The Lord is on the way to bring salvation.

There was another reason for confidence in the future. Many Jews looked forward to the coming of a future deliverer—a messiah.

Jewish Expectations for a Messiah

For Christians, the identity of the "Messiah" is not in question—he is Jesus, the "Son of God." Jewish expectations at the time of Jesus, however, were quite diverse.[1] Jewish groups disagreed about many things, including what the future would bring (cf. Acts 23:6). If we truly want to enter into the Christmas story, we need to understand how Jewish messianic expectations in Jesus' day were being shaped.

An Anointed One

The Hebrew word translated "messiah" (*mashiyach*) simply means "anointed one." In the Scriptures of Israel, various

---

1 See the important studies in Matthew V. Novenson, *The Grammar of Messianism: An Ancient Jewish Political Idiom and Its Users* (Oxford: Oxford University Press, 2017); John Collins, *The Scepter and the Star: The Messiahs of the Dead Sea Scrolls and Other Ancient Literature* (New York: Doubleday, 1995).

kinds of people were anointed, including priests (Exodus 28:41; 30:30; 40:13, 15; Leviticus 16:32) and prophets (1 Kings 19:16; Isaiah 61:1). Most prominently, however, Israel's king was known as the "anointed one."

A famous example of a royal anointing is found in the Old Testament story of God's choice of David as king. When he is anointed by the prophet Samuel, something remarkable happens to David. We are told:

> Then Samuel took the horn of oil, and *anointed him* in the midst of his brothers, and *the Spirit of the LORD came mightily upon David* from that day on. (1 Samuel 16:13)

Here an important connection is made: the king is anointed with oil, which symbolizes the anointing of the Spirit of God.

In Hebrew, then, the king of Israel is often called "the LORD's anointed"—that is, "the LORD's *messiah* (Hebrew: *mashiyach*)" (e.g., 1 Samuel 24:10; 26:9, 11). In the Greek version of the Old Testament, "messiah" is translated with the Greek word for "anointed one," *christos*. To be king, then, is to be "christ."

Yet David's kingship becomes special for another reason. Because of his faithfulness, God eventually rewards David with an astounding promise. Through the prophet Nathan, the Lord tells David the following:

> When your days are completed and you lie down with your fathers, I will raise up your offspring after you.... I will establish his kingdom. He shall build a house for my name, and I shall establish the throne of his kingdom forever. I will be his father, and he shall be my son. (2 Samuel 7:12–14)

God swears to give David an *everlasting kingdom*. Moreover, the prophet announces that the son of David will also be the "son of God."

In some ways, Nathan's oracle would seem to be fulfilled in the glorious reign of David's son, Solomon. Solomon built a splendid temple, fulfilling God's promise that David's son would "build a house" for the Lord. Yet Solomon did not reign forever. In fact, the kingdom of David came to a sudden end when the Babylonians conquered Jerusalem in 587 B.C. After that, no more kings from David's line would rule over the people.

By the time of Jesus' birth, it had been close to 600 years since a descendant of David had ruled over Israel. Yet Jews knew the promise God had made to David: his kingdom would last *forever*. This gave rise to Jewish hopes that the Lord would keep the promise made to David by raising up a future king from his line. This would be the definitive king—the "Messiah" par excellence.

Messianic Prophecies

Messianic hopes took various forms at the time of Jesus. The Dead Sea Scrolls reveal that some Jews, for example, were anticipating the coming of a *priestly* leader from the line of Israel's first high priest, Aaron.[2] Some Jews seem to have expected more than one messiah—a royal one and a priestly one. Nevertheless, the most dominant strain of Jewish hopes for the future involved the coming of a king from the line of David. Such beliefs were rooted in various prophecies.

For example, in Isaiah we read:

A shoot shall come out from the stump of Jesse,
and a branch shall grow out of his roots.
The spirit of the LORD shall rest on him,
the spirit of wisdom and understanding. . . .
With righteousness he shall judge the poor,

---

2   Damascus Document 14:18–19.

> and decide with equity for the meek of the earth;
> he shall strike the earth with the rod of his mouth,
> and with the breath of his lips he shall kill the wicked.
>   (Isaiah 11:1–2, 4)

Jesse was King David's father. By speaking not of the "tree of Jesse," but of the "stump of Jesse," Isaiah suggests that David's line has been "chopped down" by Israel's enemies. This is what happened when the Babylonians invaded Jerusalem in 587 B.C.—the Davidic kingdom came to an end, and the Jews went off into exile.

Nevertheless, Isaiah's prophecy contains a message of hope: a "branch" is seen coming from the "stump" of Jesse. The meaning of the symbolism is unmistakable: God will yet again raise up a king from David's royal line. This figure will come in the Spirit of God, judge with righteousness, and defeat the wicked "with the rod of his mouth and with the breath of his lips"—that is, with his words. He will come with "wisdom," an attribute famously associated with Solomon (see 1 Kings 4:29–34).

Today, some Christians have the devotional practice of preparing for Christmas by making a "Jesse Tree." This can take different forms. Regardless of how it is done, its purpose is to recall the way Jesus represents the fulfillment of Scripture.

According to Isaiah, the future descendant of David will usher in an age in which God will bring unprecedented peace. Not only will the people of Israel have rest from their enemies, but the world will return to a harmony among God's creatures reminiscent of the Garden of Eden:

> Then a wolf shall dwell with a lamb,
> and a leopard shall lie down with a young goat,
> and a calf and a lion and a fatling together,
> and a little child shall guide them. (Isaiah 11:6)

Isaiah and other prophets speak of the age of Israel's restoration in terms of a "new creation" (Isaiah 66:22). As we shall see, this will become a key factor in the Christmas story of Jesus' birth.

When the Son of God Appears

Hopes for a messiah were also fueled by other Scriptures. For example, various psalms speak of the day God will bring definitive victory over evil through a son of David. We read about how the nations conspire "against the LORD and against his Anointed One" (Psalm 2:2)—literally, the "Messiah" or "Christ." The king says:

> The LORD said to me, "You are my Son;
>   today I have begotten you.
> Ask from me, and I will make the nations your inheritance,
>   and the ends of the earth your possession.
> You shall break them with a rod of iron
>   and shatter them like a potter's vessel." (Psalm 2:7–9)

Here, like Solomon, the unnamed king is described as God's "son." While the psalm was likely written to honor the enthronement of a historical king, it represents a view of an idealized ruler that no historical figure completely realized. When David's kingdom came to an end, psalms like this one took on new meaning and were reread as expressing hopes for a *future* king. These psalms were understood as referring to *the* Anointed One, *the* "Messiah" or "Christ."

Other passages also inspired messianic hopes. In Isaiah, we find a description of a coming child who will rule God's people. Its words will be familiar to those who know the musical masterpiece composed by George Frideric Handel in 1741:

> For unto us a child is born,
> unto us a son is given;
> and the government shall be upon his shoulder,
> and his name shall be called
> Wonderful Counselor, Mighty God,
> Everlasting Father, Prince of Peace.
> Of the increase of his dominion and of peace
> there will be no end,
> on the throne of David and over his kingdom,
> to establish it and to sustain it
> with justice and with righteousness
> now and for forever. (Isaiah 9:6–7)

Within the book of Isaiah, there are good reasons to believe that this "Prince of Peace" refers in some way to the righteous king Hezekiah, who emerges as a key character in later chapters. Isaiah gives the future ruler the further title "Mighty God." Though Hezekiah was not *actually* God, it was said that "the LORD was with him" (2 Kings 18:7). Hezekiah, then, can be seen as a *partial* fulfillment to this prophecy.

Still, Hezekiah did not fully realize Isaiah's grand vision for a "Prince of Peace." Under him, justice was not established "for forever" (Isaiah 9:7). The oracle could therefore also be read as pointing to a future king.[3]

The book of Isaiah also contains the prophecy that informs the lyrics "O Come, O Come Emmanuel." In one place, Isaiah speaks of the birth of a child named "Immanuel," which in Hebrew means "God with us" (Isaiah 7:14). (In Hebrew, the word "Immanuel" begins with the equivalent of the letter "I." In Greek and Latin, the word translated "Emmanuel" begins with the equivalent of the letter "E". So, when we are talking

---

3   See Adela Yarbro Collins and John J. Collins, *King and Messiah as Son of God: Divine, Human, and Angelic Messianic Figures in Biblical and Related Literature* (Grand Rapids, MI: Eerdmans, 2008), 42–43.

about the passage in the original book of Isaiah, the name is written as "Immanuel," and when we are talking about the New Testament's use of the prophecy, which is written in Greek, we use "Emmanuel.")

Like the passage above, scholars believe that within the book of Isaiah the prophecy of an Immanuel child also refers in some way to King Hezekiah.[4] But, again, Hezekiah does not bring about lasting peace. The prophecy can therefore have a future meaning. As we shall see, the New Testament will find in Jesus the ultimate realization of Isaiah's oracle.

Freedom from Sin

As Moses explained, Israel was exiled because of sin. Restoration from exile was therefore connected with hopes for the forgiveness of sin and atonement. For ancient Jews, these ideas were bound up with another concept: redemption.

The Angel Gabriel and the Jubilee

In the Jewish Scriptures, it is often understood that Israel's exile was not simply due to the problem of Gentile sinners; the people must turn to God and be saved from their *own* sin. The book of Daniel emphasizes this. Speaking on behalf of Israel, Daniel prays, "We have sinned and done wrong and acted wickedly. . . . And the curse and the oath which are written in the law of Moses the servant of God have been poured out upon us, because we have sinned" (Daniel 9:5, 11).

After Daniel completes this prayer, something remarkable happens: the angel Gabriel—a key figure in the story of Jesus'

---

4   Christopher Seitz, *Isaiah 1–39*, Interpretation (Louisville: Westminster John Knox Press, 1993), 64–65.

birth in the New Testament—appears to the prophet. The angel makes a stirring announcement: God's people will be delivered. This news is proclaimed in highly symbolic terms:

> Seventy weeks of years are decreed about your people and your holy city, to finish transgression, to make an end to sin, and to atone for iniquity, to bring in everlasting righteousness. (Daniel 9:24)

Gabriel announces that Israel's redemption will come after "seventy weeks of years." This time frame evokes the Jewish notion of the "Jubilee" year. It is important to understand what this meant to ancient Israel.[5]

Just as God declared that the seventh day, Saturday, was the Sabbath, the holy day of rest (Exodus 20:8–10), so also every seventh year was considered a "Sabbath year." During this year, the Israelites were to let their land lie fallow and give it rest (Leviticus 25:1–7). Furthermore, after every seven Sabbath years—that is, after forty-nine years (7×7 years)—Israel was to celebrate the "Jubilee year" (Leviticus 25:8–55). In Daniel, Gabriel says Israel's restoration will come after "seventy weeks of years." This is a Jubilee image. Since there are seven days in a week, "seventy weeks of years" means 70×7, or 490 years. Gabriel has announced the coming of the *great* Jubilee celebration. But why was the Jubilee so important?

The Jubilee, Debts, and the Forgiveness of Sins

The Jubilee year effectively wiped out all consequences of debt. In ancient Israel, too much debt could force people to

---

5   My discussion here is based on the fuller scholarship found in John S. Bergsma, *The Jubilee from Leviticus to Qumran: A History of Interpretation* (Leiden: Brill, 2007).

sell their ancestral land (Leviticus 25:25–34). Even worse, debt could cause people to be sold into slavery (Leviticus 25:39–55; cf. 2 Kings 4:1–7). In the Jubilee year, however, all of these consequences were reversed. Slaves were set free, and lands were returned to their original owners. (Anyone with a mortgage or with student or credit-card debt would welcome a Jubilee today.)

The Jubilee was an appropriate symbol for Israel's restoration for another reason. As I explain in my previous book *Salvation*, Jews came to view sin as a kind of spiritual debt to God.[6] We see this metaphor for sin in the Lord's Prayer, the Our Father. Jesus teaches his disciples to pray, "Forgive us our *debts*, as we also have forgiven our *debtors*" (Matthew 6:12). Here sin is conceived of as a debt.

The Jubilee year was an appropriate image for Israel's deliverance from exile. The people's debt of sin was what put them in exile in the first place. Restoration would have to involve the forgiveness of that sin-debt. Gabriel thus links the "seventy weeks of years"—that is, the Jubilee—to the announcement that this period will "make an end to sin" (Daniel 9:24). In fact, the Jubilee year was supposed to be proclaimed on the Day of Atonement (Leviticus 25:9), the very festival that dealt with atonement for *sin* (cf. Leviticus 16:30). It is worth mentioning that the language of "atoning" had an economic connotation; among other things, it could refer to paying a "ransom" price.[7] If you were a slave due to debt, you could be "redeemed"—set free—if someone paid the price of your debt.

We can now bring all the threads we have been discussing together. For ancient Jews, debt, sin, slavery, and atonement

---

6   See the discussion and sources in Michael Patrick Barber, *Salvation: What Every Catholic Should Know* (San Francisco: Ignatius Press; Greenwood Village, CO: Augustine Institute, 2019), 37–52. While the book is especially written for Catholics, it aims to be helpful for all Christians.

7   See Brant Pitre, Michael Barber, and John Kincaid, *Paul, a New Covenant Jew: Rethinking Pauline Theology* (Grand Rapids, MI: Eerdmans, 2019), 145–49.

could all be seen as related ideas. The people of Israel were *enslaved* by their enemies in the exile because of their *debt* of sin. It is no surprise given the Jubilee imagery, then, that Gabriel tells Daniel that "seventy weeks of years" have been "decreed" in order "*to put an end to sin*, and *to atone for iniquity*" (Daniel 9:24).

The Jubilee and Hopes for a Messiah

Gabriel's Jubilee announcement to Daniel also involves the vision of a coming "anointed one, a prince" (Daniel 9:25). In fact, other Jewish sources speak of an "anointed one" coming as part of Israel's future Jubilee restoration. Take, for example, this passage from the book of Isaiah:

> The Spirit of the Lord GOD is upon me,
> because *the LORD has anointed me*;
> he has sent me to bring good news to the oppressed,
> to bind up the brokenhearted,
> to proclaim *liberty to the captives*,
> and *release to those who are bound*;
> to proclaim *the year of the LORD's favor*. (Isaiah 61:1–2)

Here we see three important ideas. First, Isaiah announces the coming of a figure who is "anointed" by the Spirit. From the Dead Sea Scrolls, we see that ancient Jews interpreted this passage as referring to the Messiah.[8] Second, the anointed one announces "liberty" for "captives" and "release to those who are bound." In other words, those who are enslaved will be set free. Third, that this future salvation is connected to the Jubilee year is confirmed in the last line: all of this takes

---

8 4QMessianic Apocalypse (4Q= Qumran, Cave 4).

place as part of *"the year of the LORD's favor"*—a reference to the Jubilee.

In the New Testament, Isaiah's prophecy is shown to be fulfilled in Jesus. In the synagogue at Nazareth, Jesus reads the very passage quoted above from Isaiah. After he is done, he stuns the congregation by declaring, "Today this Scripture has been fulfilled in your hearing" (Luke 4:21). Jesus is the Messiah. Through him, the definitive Jubilee promised by Isaiah is realized.

Israel's Hopes and Our Hopes

The discussion above explains the first verse of the famous hymn "O Come, O Come, Emmanuel." The song asks God to "ransom captive Israel," which "mourns in lonely exile." It goes on to explain that Israel's plight will end when "the Son of God"—the Messiah—arrives. At Christmas we rejoice because, as the New Testament reveals, these hopes are realized in Jesus, the Messiah, the Christ.

Israel longed to return home. They yearned to be free from exile and find peace. Yet many in Israel understood that only God would be able to bring about their definitive salvation. They needed a deliverer to free them from the consequences of their sin.

And so do all of us.

In a way, we all seek what ancient Israel did. Christmas highlights such longings. We might reflect on ways we feel "exiled." We can recall Christmases of the past when we laughed and played with the joy of childhood innocence. Parents and children remember with tenderness experiencing Christmas with one another. Watching old home videos of past Christmases can be emotional because we sometimes see in them better times. There might also be sadness over broken relationships.

Sin destroys our relationships. It leads to broken homes and broken lives. It leads to separation from the God who loves us. We long for peace and to be saved from the shattering effects of our sinfulness.

Christmas, however, tells us that a deliverer has come. We truly can be "ransomed" from our guilt. We can come home in Christ, the true Emmanuel—"God with us." This is not simply about an individualistic salvation either. It involves sharing in the promises made to God's people, Israel. God does not simply save *this* person or *that* person; to be saved means being part of the people of God. But to understand how that is possible, we need to have a firmer grasp on who Christ is. To discover that, we now turn to the New Testament.

3

"Tidings of Comfort and Joy": Gabriel's Announcement to Zechariah

One of the most well-known Christmas songs is "God Rest Ye Merry Gentlemen." The song, whose origin may be as early as the 1500s and whose composer is unknown, begins:

> God rest ye merry gentlemen
> Let nothing you dismay
> Remember Christ Our Savior
> Was born on Christmas Day
> To save us all from Satan's pow'r
> When we were had astray
> Oh tidings of comfort and joy
> Comfort and joy
> Oh tidings of comfort and joy.

Who are these "merry gentlemen"? Why might they be "dismayed"? What precisely were the "tidings of comfort and joy"? Here I want to look at how the message of the hymn is exemplified by the story that opens the Gospel of Luke.[1] The angel Gabriel—the angel we read about in the last chapter—returns

---

1   In this book I refer to the Gospels' writers by their traditional names without prejudice to the debates about the question of their authorship.

once again to make another announcement: God is about to deliver Israel.

The first person to hear about *how* this will happen is a priest named Zechariah. He receives the news as "tidings of comfort and joy." The coming of the Messiah is an answer to his prayers—but in ways he could have never expected.

Zechariah's Temple Service and Gabriel's Appearance

After a brief prologue, Luke introduces some of the pivotal people in his account of Jesus' birth. We read:

> In the days of Herod, king of Judea, there was a certain priest named Zechariah, of the priestly division of Abijah. His wife was from the daughters of Aaron, and her name was Elizabeth. They were both righteous before God, walking in all the commandments and legal requirements of the Lord blamelessly. But they had no child because Elizabeth was barren, and they were both advanced in years. (Luke 1:5–7)

Who is Herod? And what is so important about Zechariah and Elizabeth? Why does Luke begin his account of Jesus' birth with these people?

Zechariah, the Righteous Priest

The scene opens with the mention of King Herod the Great. The Gospel writer does not say much about him; that would not have been necessary. The original readers of Luke would have known all about Herod. Everyone in the region of Jerusalem lived under his tyrannical reign. He was well known for his ambition and ruthless quest for power. He had three of his own sons killed when he became concerned that they might represent a threat to him. He also killed his wife, her mother, and her brother. Suffice it to say, his cruelty was well known.[2]

Zechariah and his wife, Elizabeth, serve as photographic negatives of Herod. In contrast to Herod's legendary sinfulness, the elderly priest and his wife are said to be "righteous" (*dikaioi*). Luke informs us that they faithfully follow "all the commandments" of the Lord "blamelessly" (Luke 1:6). Whereas Herod is a powerful ruler, Zechariah is a lowly priest. It may seem as if the righteous have been abandoned by God, while evil reigns supreme. But God has a plan.

Zechariah and the Tamid Sacrifice

It is important to the story that Zechariah is a priest. In fact, Luke provides some important details about the setting of Zechariah's priestly service.

> Now it happened that while he was serving as priest before God when his division was on duty, according to the custom of the priesthood, he was chosen by lot to go into the temple of the Lord to burn incense. And the whole multitude of the people was praying outside at the hour of the incense offering. (Luke 1:8–10)

In the first century, there were around 20,000 Jewish priests.[3] The various priestly families were divided up into different groups and each served at different times of the year

2   For a recent summary treatment, see Benedikt Eckhardt, "Herod the Great," in *T&T Clark Encyclopedia of Second Temple Judaism*, ed. Daniel M. Gurtner and Loren T. Struckenbruck, 2 vols. (London: T&T Clark, 2019), 2:335–337.

3   See Josephus, *Apion* 2.108, and discussion in E. P. Sanders, *Judaism: Practice and Belief, 63 BCE–66 CE* (London: SCM Press, 1992), 78–79.

(1 Chronicles 24:4). Zechariah is serving in the temple not because he is high priest but as part of the usual rotation of the priestly families.

The ritual Luke describes Zechariah performing is part of the *Tamid* offering (pronounced *tah-MEED*). Regulations for this rite can be found in the Torah (cf. Exodus 29:38–42; Numbers 28:3–8) and in later Jewish works (see Mishnah Tamid). In Hebrew, *Tamid* means "continual," which was an appropriate name for the ritual since it was repeated twice every day.

Luke's account of Zechariah's activity in the sanctuary and the detail that "the whole multitude of the people were praying outside" (Luke 1:10) fits with what we know about the way the *Tamid* was carried out in Jesus' day. Jews would gather outside the temple in prayer while they waited for the priests to complete the offering. When it was finished, a priestly blessing was imparted to the crowd. For Jews in Jerusalem, the daily *Tamid* offering "was the primary liturgy of the temple."[4]

Gabriel, Daniel, and Zechariah

When Zechariah enters the temple, he is startled to find that he is not alone there: "Then there appeared to him an angel of the Lord, standing at the right side of the altar of incense" (Luke 1:11). When Zechariah sees the angel, he is afraid. In the Bible, those who encounter angels are often struck by fear (Numbers 22:31; Daniel 10:7). Angelic beings are often the agents of divine judgment (Isaiah 37:36; Psalm 78:49).

---

4   Dennis Hamm, "The Tamid Service in Luke-Acts: The Cultic Background behind Luke's Theology of Worship (Luke 1:5–25; 18:9–14; 24:50–53; Acts 3:1; 10:3, 30)," *Catholic Biblical Quarterly* 25 (2003): 216.

Zechariah may have recalled that angels had scourged the evil Heliodorus to the point of death when he entered the temple unworthily (2 Maccabees 3:22–34).

Furthermore, we learn that this is not just any angel. He later reveals to Zechariah: "I am *Gabriel*" (Luke 1:19). This is the *same angel* who announced the great Jubilee to the prophet Daniel. In fact, Gabriel appears by name in only three places in the Bible—in Daniel, where he announces the future Jubilee restoration of Israel, and in Luke's accounts of Zechariah and Mary.

Moreover, notice that Gabriel comes to Zechariah at *the exact same time* he once appeared to Daniel—at the time of the *Tamid*. In Daniel, we read: "Gabriel ... came to me in flight *at the time of the evening sacrifice*" (Daniel 9:21). As a priest, Zechariah himself performs the very ritual, the *Tamid*, that was the backdrop for Gabriel's original announcement in Daniel. Yet whereas Gabriel tells Daniel that what he prays for—the salvation of Israel—will only occur in the distant future, Zechariah hears a different message: the time of salvation is finally at hand.

The God Who Answers Prayers

The angel makes a momentous announcement to Zechariah:

> Do not be afraid, Zechariah, for your prayer has been heard, and your wife Elizabeth will bear you a son, and you shall call his name John. And you will have joy and gladness, and many will rejoice at his birth; for he will be great before the Lord. (Luke 1:13–15)

Zechariah is told "your prayer has been heard." But for what had he been praying?

Zechariah's Son as Herald of the Messiah

When Zechariah goes into the temple, he is likely not merely praying for himself. The time of the *Tamid* offering was associated with prayers for the forgiveness of Israel's sin and for the nation's future restoration (Ezra 9:5–7; Judith 9:1–14). It is natural to assume his prayer would include such intentions.

Yet God fulfills Zechariah's prayers in an unexpected way: not only does the priest learn that Israel will be delivered, but he is told that this will occur in a way he never could have anticipated—he and his wife will have a miraculous child in their old age. Zechariah is told to name him "John" (Luke 1:13). Of course, Zechariah's son is none other than John the Baptist, the man who announces Jesus' coming and baptizes him.

Gabriel goes on to describe to Zechariah who John will be:

> For he shall be great before the Lord, and shall drink neither wine nor strong drink. And he shall be filled with the Holy Spirit while he is still in his mother's womb. And he shall turn many of the children of Israel to the Lord their God. And he shall go before him in the spirit and power of Elijah, to turn the hearts of the fathers to the children, and the disobedient to the wisdom of the righteous; to make ready a people prepared for the Lord. (Luke 1:15–17)

Here let us pause to reflect on two important ideas found in Gabriel's announcement.

First, Gabriel says John will not drink "wine" or "strong drink." This is an allusion to the Jewish practice of the Nazirite vow (Numbers 6:3). Nazirites consecrated themselves to the Lord. They expressed this consecration by not cutting their hair (Numbers 6:5). In the Scriptures, biblical heroes Samson and Samuel are said to be Nazirites from birth

(Judges 13:4–5; 1 Samuel 1:11). John the Baptist will be like them. That he will be a Nazirite like Samuel is especially fitting. It was Samuel who anointed David. If you recall from the previous chapter, when this happened the Spirit of God descended upon David. This foreshadows what happens later in the Gospel of Luke—when John baptizes Jesus, the true Son of David, "the Holy Spirit descended upon him in bodily form" (Luke 3:22). The following chart helps to visualize the relationship between Samuel and John.

Samuel	John the Baptist
Nazirite	Nazirite
Anoints King David	Baptizes Jesus the Messiah

Just as the Nazirite Samuel anoints David, so the Nazirite John baptizes the Messiah.

Second, Gabriel reveals that John will go "in the spirit and power of Elijah, to turn the hearts of the fathers to the children" (Luke 1:17). This part of Gabriel's announcement is taken from an Old Testament prophecy. In the book of Malachi, God promises to send the prophet Elijah to prepare the people for the day of the Lord's arrival:

> Behold, I will send you Elijah the prophet before the great and terrible day of the LORD comes. And he will *turn the hearts of fathers to their children and the hearts of children to their fathers,* lest I come and smite the land with a curse. (Malachi 4:5–6; cf. Sirach 48:10)

Repentance must involve repairing broken relationships. This involves parents turning their hearts to their children, and children likewise seeking reconciliation with their parents.

Gabriel reveals John the Baptist to be the *new Elijah*, the one who will call the people to turn from sin. Going out to the wilderness, John proclaims "a baptism of repentance for the forgiveness of sins" (Luke 3:3).

Zechariah's Unbelief

Upon hearing the angel's announcement, Zechariah is incredulous: "How shall I know this?" he asks, pointing out that he and his wife are elderly (Luke 1:18). Zechariah is *unable* to believe that he can have a son. As a result, he ends up mute. The angel tells him why: "because you did not believe" (Luke 1:20). After his son is born, however, his voice is restored to him. Out of faithfulness, he does what the angel tells him and insists, against his extended family's wishes, on naming the child John (Luke 1:57–64). When his tongue is loosed, he proceeds to bless and extol the Lord (Luke 1:68–79).

Prepare the Way of the Lord

Yet God does more than just hear Zechariah's prayers—he goes beyond them. His son, John the Baptist, is not simply described as preparing the way of the *Messiah*. The careful reader will recognize that the word "Christ" or "Messiah" is never explicitly used by Gabriel when he speaks to Zechariah. Instead, Zechariah is told that his son "shall turn many of the children of Israel to *the Lord their God*. And he shall go before *him*" (Luke 1:16–17). Who is it that John is going before? Not simply the "Messiah" but "the Lord their God." In this, Jesus' full identity is subtly revealed to the reader. To appreciate how this is the case, we must once again read the story with a Jewish mindset.

The Birth of the Lord

Out of concern to keep the commandment "You shall not take the name of the LORD your God in vain" (Exodus 20:7), Jews avoided using the name of God. Of course, that holy name was revealed to Moses at the burning bush. It is transliterated into English as "YHWH" (there are no vowels in ancient Hebrew). In its place, ancient Jews would substitute the term "Lord."[5] This practice is evident in the Dead Sea Scrolls, where the Hebrew word for "Lord" is sometimes written above the divine name. Likewise, the ancient Jewish writer Philo uses the Greek word for "Lord" (*kyrios*) rather than writing out the divine name. The ancient Greek translation of the Old Testament, the Septuagint, does the same. This custom is continued in English Bible translations today. Rather than writing out God's name, English translations of the Old Testament render it with "LORD" (in small capital letters).

The Gospel of Luke is written in Greek. When Luke quotes from Old Testament passages that use the divine name, he follows Jewish tradition. Instead of writing out the Greek equivalent of "YHWH," he uses the Greek term for "Lord" (Greek: *kyrios*). Take, for example, Luke's quotation of Isaiah's line: "Prepare the way of the LORD" (Isaiah 40:3). The original Hebrew has "YHWH." When Luke quotes this passage, he uses the normal Greek word for "Lord" (Greek: *kyrios*). There are enormous implications in all of this for understanding Jesus' identity.

As New Testament scholar C. Kavin Rowe has shown, by calling Jesus "Lord," Luke reveals that Jesus is to be identified with the God of Israel.[6] For instance, later in the Gospel, Elizabeth says the following to Mary, the mother of Jesus:

---

5   For further discussion, see Brant Pitre, Michael P. Barber, and John A. Kincaid, *Paul, a New Covenant Jew: Rethinking Pauline Theology* (Grand Rapids, MI: Eerdmans, 2019), 111–13.

6   C. Kavin Rowe, *Early Narrative Christology: The Lord in the Gospel of Luke* (Berlin: Walter de Gruyter, 2006).

> Blessed are you among women and blessed is the fruit of
> your womb. And how is this granted to me, that *the mother*
> *of my Lord* should come to me? Behold, when the sound of
> your greeting came to my ears the babe in my womb leaped
> for joy. And blessed is she who believed that there will be a
> fulfillment to what was spoken to her from the *Lord*. (Luke
> 1:42–43)

This is a remarkable passage.

Notice that Elizabeth refers to Mary not simply as the
"mother of the Christ" but as "the mother of my *Lord* [Greek:
hē mētēr tou kyriou]" (Luke 1:43). Here Mary's role as mother
of the Christ is surely affirmed; the Messiah was a king and,
therefore, could be called "lord." Yet Luke probably intends
something more here.

Up until this point in the narrative, "Lord" has been used
for the God of Israel ten times. Moreover, Elizabeth goes on
to say that Mary is "blessed" because she believed "what was
spoken ... from the *Lord* [Greek: *para kyriou*]" (Luke 1:45).
In context, "Lord" refers to the God of Israel. But now suddenly Elizabeth speaks of Mary as "the mother of my *Lord*,"
identifying Jesus with this title. Rowe calls this "the most startling verse in the birth-infancy narrative and perhaps in the
entire Gospel."[7] Jesus is not only the Messiah, but he is also
identified as the Lord, the God of Israel.

The Word-Made-Flesh

Jesus' divine identity is further emphasized later in Luke's narrative in various ways. Perhaps most striking is Jesus' saying,
"Why do you call me 'Lord, Lord [*kyrie, kyrie*],' and not do

---

7   Ibid., 39.

what I tell you?" (Luke 6:46). A similar saying appears in the Gospel of Matthew (Matthew 7:21). New Testament scholar Jason Staples shows that this usage of "Lord" should be understood as implying Jesus' identity as the God of Israel. By itself "lord" need not refer to God—it can, for example, refer to kings. Yet Staples shows that the *double usage*, "Lord, Lord," is *exclusively* used for the God of Israel in the Greek version of the Old Testament.[8]

The description of Zechariah's son as one who goes "before the Lord" (Luke 1:15) tells us as much about Jesus as it does about John the Baptist. God is fulfilling messianic hopes in a way that no one could have anticipated. Isaiah spoke of a coming figure who would be called "mighty God" (Isaiah 9:6) and "Immanuel," which means "God with us" (Isaiah 7:14). In Christ, these prophecies are fulfilled in a way that went beyond expectations; God comes in the flesh.

For many, the notion that the Almighty God would become human was scandalous. According to some, the material world *itself* was to be despised. There were those who believed human fulfillment could only be found in separating the human soul from the body and material elements. The doctrine of the Incarnation—God taking "flesh" (Latin: *caro, carnis*)—emphasizes a truth proclaimed in the book of Genesis, namely, that the material world is created "good." God does not despise materiality. The human body is not a prison to be liberated from or merely a "husk" to be discarded. As the Gospel of John would say, Christ is the "Word of God" who "was God" (John 1:1). And this Word "became flesh" (John 1:14) to save the world (John 3:16).

In Luke's narrative, it is unlikely that Zechariah and Elizabeth fully grasp what it means that John will go "before the

---

8   Jason Staples, "'Lord, LORD': Jesus as YHWH in Matthew and Luke," *New Testament Studies* 64 (2018): 1–19.

Lord" (Luke 1:16–17). Richard Hays, a noted New Testament scholar, correctly says, "Jesus' identity unfolds *cumulatively* through the Gospel."[9] As Luke's narrative continues, the reader better understands why Jesus is called "Lord."

Lessons for Christmas

What have we seen here? First, God answers prayers. The same angel who announces to Daniel the coming Jubilee restoration of Israel appears again in the Gospel of Luke to reveal that the time of deliverance is at hand. In this, Zechariah's prayers—and the prayers of Jews like Daniel—are finally realized; a Messiah is coming.

Second, because the Messiah is coming, relationships can be healed. As Malachi announced, the hearts of parents will be turned to their children and the hearts of children will be turned to their parents. Sin and its effects are finally dealt with in the coming of Christ.

Third, God answers Zechariah's prayers in ways that transcend his highest hopes. Not only did God answer Zechariah's prayers for the redemption of Israel, but the priest learns that this will occur through a son whom his wife will miraculously conceive in her old age. The Messiah is finally coming, and he will be heralded by Zechariah's own extraordinary child. At first, Zechariah finds this hard to believe and airs his doubts. Yet, as he comes to see, the promises of God come true. Indeed, the identity of Jesus further emphasizes the way God goes beyond our expectations. Not only is the Messiah on his way, but the Messiah *himself* is the Lord. Jesus is a Messiah greater than that which could have been anticipated.

---

9   Richard Hays, *Echoes of Scripture in the Gospels* (Waco, TX: Baylor University Press, 2018), 244; emphasis in original.

There are lessons here for all of us. At Christmas, as we celebrate the birth of the promised Messiah, we recall that God answers prayers. Above all, the reconciliation and restoration Israel longed for has come in Christ the Savior. Moreover, in Christ, families can be healed, and sin can be overcome. We have nothing to dismay! What the story of Gabriel's announcement to Zechariah makes clear is that God can do even more than we believe is possible. As Gabriel will tell Mary, "with God nothing will be impossible" (Luke 1:37).

Yet we must add a further point: our hopes can be realized, but only if we conform them to God's will. Insisting on having things our way will lead us to be forever disappointed at Christmas. God answers our prayers but not always in ways we expect. Sometimes it may seem—as it did to Zechariah—that certain things are impossible with God. The birth of John—and ultimately, the birth of Jesus—shows us this is not the case. Those who trust in the Lord will never be let down. Even if things do not work out the way we expect them to, God has better plans than we do. Faith means believing that this is true. Christmas celebrates that God is true to his word and fulfills our hopes in ways that exceed them.

After Gabriel's announcement to Zechariah, we next read about another visit the angel makes. This time, unlike Zechariah, the person Gabriel appears to responds properly—that is, with faith. We now consider Mary's role in the Christmas story.

4

"Christ Is Born of Mary": Gabriel's Announcement to Mary

One of the most beloved Christmas carols is "O Little Town of Bethlehem." The song begins with a beautifully poetic description of Jesus' birthplace:

> Oh little town of Bethlehem
> How still we see thee lie
> Above thy deep and dreamless sleep
> The silent stars go by.

After setting the scene, the song focuses on Jesus' birth: "Christ is born of Mary."

When we think of the nativity, we first think of the Christ child—the Messiah. After Jesus, we mention Mary. No depiction of the nativity is truly complete without her. In portrayals of the nativity, we often find some mix of angels, shepherds, magi, oxen, donkeys, lambs, and the star of Bethlehem. Joseph is usually present, though he is sometimes relegated to the background. But Mary is usually not hard to find. She is usually close to the infant King.

That "O Little Town of Bethlehem" uses the phrase "*Christ is born of Mary*" is significant. As we have shown, the term points to Jesus' identity as the long-awaited Messiah. As the song "O Little Town of Bethlehem" says of the village,

"The hopes and fears of all the years / Are met in thee tonight."
As Mary looked upon her child, she saw not only her baby,
but the one who had come to deliver her people.

Or did she?

According to the popular song "Mary, Did You Know?,"
Mary was ignorant of Jesus' identity. The song asks Mary a
series of questions such as,

> Mary, did you know that your baby boy would save our sons
>   and daughters?
> Did you know that your baby boy has come to make you new?
> This child that you've delivered, will soon deliver you.

Strangely, the song never mentions an important New Testament scene: in the Gospel of Luke, the angel Gabriel comes
to Mary and explicitly tells her about the child she is to bear.

Here we will look more carefully at what Luke says Gabriel
told Mary. Who does Gabriel say Mary's child will be? *How*
will he be conceived? And what does this mean for us today?
Only by looking closely at Luke's account will we be able to
see why Mary is such an important part of the Christmas story.

Christ the Lord

When Gabriel appears to Mary in Luke, he makes it very clear
who her son will be—he will be the Messiah. But how does
Gabriel reveal this?

Mother of the Son of David

Gabriel tells Mary:

> And behold, you shall conceive in the womb and give birth
> to a son, and shall call his name Jesus. He shall be great, and

shall be called *the Son of the Most High*, and *the Lord God shall give to him the throne of David his father*. And he shall reign over the house of Jacob forever; and *of his kingdom there shall be no end*. (Luke 1:31–33)

The angel's announcement borrows several words and concepts from a crucial Old Testament prophecy. As we saw in chapter 2, through the prophet Nathan God promised to give David an everlasting kingdom. As the Dead Sea Scrolls make clear, Jews in Jesus' day believed this promise pointed to the coming of a royal messiah.[1] Consider the parallels between Nathan's prophecy and what Gabriel says to Mary:

Nathan's Prophetic Oracle to David (2 Samuel 7)	Gabriel's Announcement to Mary (Luke 1)
God will give David's son "*a great* name."	Mary's son "will be *great*."
God will seat David's son on "*the throne* of his kingdom."	Mary's son will be given "*the throne* of his father David."
God says David's son "will be my *son*."	Mary's son will be "the *Son of the Most High*."
God promises David that "your *house* and your *kingdom* shall be made sure *forever*."	Mary's son "will reign over the *house* of Jacob *forever*; and of his *kingdom* there will be no end."
(2 Samuel 7:9, 13, 14, 16)	*(Luke 1:32, 33)*

Within the Jewish world of the New Testament, the meaning of Gabriel's announcement is unmistakable: Mary's son will

---

1 4QFlorilegium (4Q174).

be the Messiah. Yet there is more: as we have seen, Jesus is more than a human Messiah in the Gospel of Luke.

Son of God, Son of Mary

As we noted earlier, the royal son of David could be called God's son (Psalm 2:7). This, however, was a kind of *adopted* sonship. Solomon, for example, had a human father—David. The angel Gabriel tells Mary that she will give birth to the "Son of the Most High" (Luke 1:32). Yet Jesus is Son of God in an unheard-of way; he has no biological father. Jesus is therefore the "Son of God" par excellence. Here it is necessary to make some distinctions.

On the one hand, Luke unambiguously identifies Jesus as human. Aside from his death and burial, the surest indicator of Jesus' humanity is his birth. On the night of the nativity, Mary bears a truly human child who needs to be swaddled (Luke 2:12) and nursed (Luke 11:27). Jesus really is the "son of Mary"—a descriptor used for him in the Gospel of Mark (Mark 6:3). In this we see that Jesus is really human.

On the other hand, as we have seen, Luke indicates that Jesus is also *more* than human. As we saw in the last chapter, among other things, this is suggested by the way he is called "Lord." Moreover, that Jesus has no human father is the surest sign that he truly is the "Son of God."

Mary as Ark of the Covenant and the Divine Son

Jesus' divine nature is further reinforced by Gabriel's description of *how* she will conceive: "The Holy Spirit will *overshadow* you" (Luke 1:35). The Greek verb translated "overshadow" (*episkiazō*) is significant. It is the same word the Greek translation of the Old Testament uses to refer to God's presence in the tabernacle, the portable sanctuary that God told Moses to build in the wilderness. The Bible tells us:

And Moses was not able to enter into the tabernacle of testimony because the cloud was *overshadowing* [Greek: *epeskiazen*] it. (Exodus 40:35, LXX [Septuagint])

Here is the key point: just as God's glory overshadowed the tabernacle, the place where God was present, Gabriel now says God's Spirit will overshadow *Mary*.[2] What the tabernacle was in the Old Testament, Mary is in the New Testament. Why? Because she is not only the mother of the son of David; in her the *Lord* is present.

Luke continues to use symbolism from Israel's sacred tabernacle in describing Mary. To see this, however, we need a little more background from the Old Testament. In the Scriptures, the center of the tabernacle is its inner sanctum, the holy of holies (Exodus 26:33–35; Hebrews 9:3). There one would find the holiest vessel in Israel, the ark of the covenant. God is said to appear over it. The ark becomes known as the "mercy seat" since God's glory is made visible above it (see 2 Samuel 6:2). For instance, in the book of Exodus, the Lord says:

There I will meet with you, and from above *the mercy seat*, from between the two cherubim that are upon the ark of the testimony, *I will speak with you*. (Exodus 25:22)

In short, God meets Israel at the ark.

Because of its holiness, no one was to touch the ark. This lesson is learned most famously when David brings the ark up to Jerusalem after a decisive battle. Yet when the ark is transported to Jerusalem, it is not handled with care. Rather than carrying it on poles in accord with the directives of the Torah

---

2   Amy-Jill Levine, "Luke," in *The Jewish Annotated New Testament*, 2nd ed., ed. Amy-Jill Levine and Marc Zvi Brettler (Oxford: Oxford University Press, 2017), 110n15, 111n35.

(Numbers 7:9), those moving the ark lazily place it on a cart.
There it sits precariously until the oxen pulling the cart stum-
ble when they come to uneven ground. Suddenly realizing
that the ark may fall, a man named Uzzah does what is strictly
forbidden—he reaches out to take hold of it. He is immediately struck down and dies (2 Samuel 6:6–7). The message is
clear: the ark must be handled with the greatest of care. David
at first responds in fear and decides to leave the ark at the
house of a man named Obed-edom (2 Samuel 6:11). However, after he sees that the man's house is blessed by the ark's
presence, he decides to bring it to Jerusalem, which he does
with great reverence and joy.

Why is the ark of the covenant important to our conver-
sation here? Because Luke seems to connect Mary to it. After
the angel departs from her, Mary visits Elizabeth, the wife of
Zechariah. Luke's account of this seems to echo the story
of the ark's journey to Jerusalem at the time of David. Consider the parallels listed in the following chart:

The Ark Is Brought to Jerusalem (2 Samuel 6)	Mary Visits Elizabeth (Luke 1)
"And David *arose* and went with all the people who were with him from Baale-*judah*"	"Mary *arose* and went with haste into the hill country of *Judah*"
"[David] *blessed* the people in the name of the Lord"	"[Elizabeth] exclaimed with a loud cry, '*Blessed* are you among women'"
"[David] said, 'How can *the ark of the Lord come to me?*'"	"[Elizabeth said:] 'And why is this granted me, that *the mother of my Lord should come to me?*'"

The Ark Is Brought to Jerusalem (2 Samuel 6)	Mary Visits Elizabeth (Luke 1)
"Michal looked out the window and saw David *leaping* and dancing before the Lord"	"[Elizabeth said:] 'For behold ... the babe in my womb *leaped* for joy' "
"The ark of the LORD *remained* in the house of Obed-edom the Gittite *three months*"	"Mary *remained* with her about *three months*"
2 Samuel 6:2, 18, 9, 16, 11	Luke 1:39, 42, 43, 44, 56

The similarities between the two stories are too numerous to be unintentional. In short, it seems Mary's journey to Elizabeth's house is being compared to the ark's trip to Jerusalem.

This is extremely significant. Luke portrays Mary in terms of the tabernacle and in terms of the ark, the holiest vessel in ancient Israel. In this, Luke's narrative underscores the holiness of the one in Mary's womb—Mary will be the mother of the *Lord*. As the Lord dwelled in the tabernacle and met Israel at the ark, so now the Lord is present in Mary. Mary is therefore rightly compared to the sacred ark. God is at work in her in an unprecedented way. This is emphasized by another aspect of Gabriel's encounter with Mary.

Full of Grace

At the very sight of Gabriel, Zechariah is afraid. In contrast, Mary is not said to experience fear when she *sees* the angel. Rather, it is the angel's *greeting* that prompts a reaction from her: "But *at this word*, she was greatly perplexed and *pondered what sort of greeting this might be*" (Luke 1:29). But what has the angel said to her that is so perplexing?

Mary as "Full of Grace"

When Gabriel first speaks to Zechariah, he addresses the priest by name: "Do not be afraid, *Zechariah*" (Luke 1:13). When he comes to Mary, however, he does not greet her using her proper name. Instead, he uses an expression that Christian tradition has long seen as profoundly meaningful.

Many Bible translations render Gabriel's greeting with something like: "Hail, *favored one*" (Luke 1:28). This translation is not wrong. The Greek expression used by Gabriel does mean "favored one." Nevertheless, the word used by Gabriel in the Greek has an important connotation that "favored one" fails to capture.

The Greek term translated "favored one" is *kecharitōmenē*. This word comes from a Greek noun that has vital significance elsewhere in the Bible: *charis*. What does *charis* mean? It is the New Testament word that is typically translated "grace." For example, Paul uses *charis* when he writes: "Since all have sinned and fall short of the glory of God, they are justified by his *grace* [*charis*] as a gift, through the redemption that is in Christ Jesus" (Romans 3:23–24). According to the New Testament, salvation occurs through the "grace"—*charis*—of God.

Notably, Gabriel uses "grace" terminology a second time in his brief encounter with Mary. The angel tells her that she has "found *favor* with God" (Luke 1:30). In Greek, "favor" is *charis*. In effect, Gabriel is saying that Mary has found "grace with God."

When Jerome, the great Bible scholar of the ancient Church, translated the Bible into Latin in the 380s, he preserved the grace language that appears in Gabriel's greeting to Mary. He rendered the verse: "Hail, *full of grace*" (Latin:

gratia plena). This has become the traditional translation. It beautifully captures the way Luke's text uses "grace" terminology for Mary.

Where did Jerome get the idea that someone could be "full of grace"? Interestingly, the concept is found in another New Testament book, the Acts of the Apostles, or "Acts" for short. This book was written as a sequel to the Gospel of Luke. In Acts, we read about the first Christian martyr, Stephen. Notably, Acts describes him as "full of grace" (Acts 6:8).

Nevertheless, we should recognize that while Acts says Stephen is "full of grace" (Greek: *plērēs charitos*), it does not apply to him the specific term Gabriel uses for Mary (*kecharitōmenē*). Remarkably, the word Gabriel uses for her is never used for anyone else in the Bible. The great early Christian scholar Origen recognized this. In a homily on Luke delivered sometime between A.D. 230 and 250, he explains:

> The angel greeted Mary with a new address, which I could not find anywhere else in Scripture.... The Greek word is *kecharitōmenē*. I do not remember having read this word elsewhere in Scripture.... *This greeting was reserved for Mary alone.*[3]

Mary, then, is startled by the angel's greeting because he addresses her in an unprecedented way.

But, we might ask, what does it mean that Mary is "full of grace"?

Mary's Faith vs. Zechariah's Doubt

Luke's description of the angel's appearance to Mary sounds very similar to the previous scene in which the priest,

---

3   Origen, *Homilies on Luke and Fragments on Luke*, trans. Joseph T. Lienhard (Washington, DC: Catholic University of America Press, 2009), 26; emphasis added.

Zechariah, encounters Gabriel in the temple. Consider the following chart, which compares the two scenes:

Annunciation to Zechariah (Luke 1)	Annunciation to Mary (Luke 1)
The angel Gabriel appears	The angel Gabriel appears
Addresses Zechariah by name	Addresses Mary as "full of grace"
Zechariah is "troubled [*etarachthē*]" when he sees the angel	Mary is "perplexed [*dietarachthē*]" at the angel's greeting
"Do not be afraid"	"Do not be afraid"
"You shall call his name John"	"You shall call his name Jesus"
"How shall I know this?"	"How will this be since I do not know man?"
Fails to believe	"Let it be done to me ..."
Luke 1:11, 13, 12, 13, 13, 18, 20	*Luke 1:26, 28, 29, 30, 31, 34, 38*

The most striking difference of all is the conclusion of the two scenes: whereas Zechariah ends up mute because, as he is told, "You did not believe" (Luke 1:20), Mary responds in faith: "Let it be done to me according to your word" (Luke 1:38). We might expect the priest in the temple to be the one who responds in faith. Not so. It is the one who is "full of grace" who immediately accepts the word announced to her.

Moreover, immediately after her encounter with the angel, Mary makes the arduous journey to visit Elizabeth, presumably to assist her during her pregnancy (Luke 1:39–45). Rather than thinking of herself, Mary gives of herself, making evident the presence of God's grace in her.

The Lord Is with You

Mary's identity as "full of grace" is revealed in her faithfulness. In this, Mary is a model to believers.

The Power of Grace

Luke can be seen as describing Mary as a model for Christians. All in Christ are recipients of grace. This is stressed in the Letter to the Ephesians, which says that all believers have been "*graced* [Greek *echaritōsen*]" (Ephesians 1:6).

But what does "grace" mean? Consider what the angel says to Mary: "Hail, full of grace, *the Lord is with you*" (Luke 1:28). Mary is full of grace because the Lord is present to her. As we have seen, Luke compares Mary to the ark of the covenant. The comparison is earth-shattering—a *human* is now put on par with the sacred ark. At first, this may seem surprising, even inappropriate. Can a human person really be *that* holy? Yet this is precisely the point of Jesus' birth.

The Messiah does not come for his sake, but for ours. Christ comes not only to set us free from sin, but *to make us holy*. In the Gospel of Luke, Mary is Exhibit A of this. We should notice that the angel identifies Mary as "full of grace" even *before* she accepts the word announced to her. The title "full of grace," therefore, is not a reward for Mary's good works; rather, it expresses the gift God has bestowed on her. Later, she says, "My soul magnifies the Lord.... From now on all generations will call me blessed" (Luke 1:46, 48).

As Bible scholar Denis Farkasfalvy writes, "full of grace" is no "exaggeration."[4]

It is here that we find the most profound meaning of Christmas: the one who created the cosmos, the all-powerful Lord of the universe, demonstrates his love for humanity by becoming human. In a homily delivered on Christmas Day in A.D. 454, Leo the Great says that this "surpasses the power of human eloquence."[5] The divine Son becomes part of the family of Adam so that the fallen children of Adam can become part of the family of God. In this, true love is revealed. As the Gospel of John famously puts it: "For God so loved the world that he gave his only Son" (John 3:16). Christmas is above all else an invitation into this love by which the heavenly Savior descends from the heights of heaven to save humanity from the depths of sin. But Christ does not simply *descend* to our level; he comes down so that we can be *raised up*. In Mary, the ark, we see this in its profundity.

Mary's Example

Why is Mary capable of saying yes to the plan of God? Because she is "full of grace." What is it that leads her to go and visit Elizabeth? Again, her status as "full of grace" explains her faithfulness. Reflecting on the stories about Mary, then, can help us understand what grace can accomplish in the believer.

The same Lord who is present in Mary lives in all who are in Christ. In a homily that can be roughly dated to sometime between A.D. 397 and A.D. 430, Augustine says:

---

4   Denis Farkasfalvy, O.Cist., *The Marian Mystery: The Outline of a Mariology* (Staten Island, NY: St. Pauls, 2014), 58.

5   Leo the Great, *Sermon* 30.1, in *Sermons*, trans. Jane Patricia Freeland and Agnes Josephine Conway (Washington, DC: Catholic University of America Press, 1996), 125.

> What you marvel at in the flesh of Mary, perform in the depths of your souls. When you believe in the heart unto justice, *you conceive Christ*; and when with the lips you confess unto salvation, *you give birth to Christ*.[6]

As Augustine emphasizes elsewhere, Mary conceives Jesus in her heart by faith through grace *before* conceiving him in her womb. But the same Christ who is present to Mary is present to all those who receive his grace. In this sense, all believers "give birth to Christ." This grace is what makes faith possible. Without the help of God's grace, we are lost. But if we ask for grace, we too can respond in faith.

The hymn "Mary, Did You Know?" communicates all the wrong lessons about the mother of Jesus. Mary does not need *us* to explain to *her* what God has done. It is hard to understand how this song finds its way into churches each year. Is it a classic hymn? No; it was written relatively recently (1984). Was it written by a legendary composer? No; it was written by Protestant Christian comedian Mark Lowry.

Once one looks closely at what the New Testament says about what Mary knew, it makes it virtually impossible to see how these lyrics can be sung in churches. Although not using the precise words of the song, the Gospel of Luke tells us that an angel came and revealed to Mary exactly who her son would be—the Messiah. As a first-century Jew, Mary would have understood that the Christ would "deliver" her and the rest of God's people. In accord with books like Isaiah, Mary would likely have linked the coming restoration of Israel with the hope for a "new creation." The song asks Mary, "Did you know that your baby boy has come to make you new?" According to the Gospel of Luke, she did. Moreover, she shows us by

---

6 Augustine, *Sermon* 196.1, in *Sermons III/6 on the Liturgical Seasons*, trans. Edmund Hill (Hyde Park, NY: New City Press, 1993), 43.

her faithfulness what this looks like. Rather than instructing Mary, in humility, we can learn from her example.

But Mary is not simply called "full of grace"; she is also typically identified as the "Virgin Mary." Why is this such a prominent feature of the Christmas story? In our next chapter, we will see why it was fitting that Mary would be known as "the Virgin" and what it means for us.

5

"Round Yon Virgin": Why a *Virgin* Mother

Perhaps the most well-known Christmas hymn is "Silent Night." Its original German lyrics were written in 1818 by Joseph Mohr, an Austrian Catholic priest. The English translation of it comes from the pen of John Freeman Young:

> Silent night, holy night
> All is calm, all is bright
> Round yon Virgin, Mother and Child.

The words of this classic song have endured because of their beauty.

But what does "Round yon Virgin" mean? The word "yon" is short for "yonder." It means something like "over there." The rest of the lyrics mean that "around" ("round") Christ and Mary there is both peace ("all is calm") and the light of glory ("all is bright").

Still, why is it so important that Jesus' mother is a *virgin* after all? Here we will examine this question more closely.

A Virgin Shall Conceive

The Gospel of Matthew tells us that Jesus' Virgin Birth represents the fulfillment of a prophecy from the book of Isaiah.

Now all this took place in order to fulfill what was said by the Lord through the prophet: "Behold, a virgin shall be with child, and bear a son, and they shall call his name Emmanuel [Isaiah 7:14]," which is translated, "God with us." (Matthew 1:22–23)

Mary's virginal conception of Jesus, we are told, fulfills Isaiah's oracle that a "virgin shall be with child." But has Matthew misread this prophecy? And what is so important about it?

Questions about the Immanuel Prophecy

As we have seen, in the Old Testament God promises to give David a kingdom that will last "forever" (2 Samuel 7:12–16). By the time of the prophet Isaiah, however, that kingdom looks like it is on the brink of annihilation. Two powerful nations form a coalition against the successor to David's throne, King Ahaz. His defeat seems imminent. It is at this point that Isaiah delivers his famous Immanuel prophecy.

Isaiah tells King Ahaz:

Therefore, the Lord himself will give you a sign: Behold, a young woman shall conceive and bear a son, and shall call his name Immanuel.... For before the boy knows how to reject evil and choose good, the land whose two kings you fear will be deserted. (Isaiah 7:14, 16)

Through Isaiah, God assures King Ahaz that the kingdom of David will be saved; Ahaz's enemies will soon be brought down. A child will be born, and before he even comes of age— "before the boy knows how to reject evil and choose good"— the nations that King Ahaz is afraid of will be defeated ("the land whose two kings you fear will be deserted"). In short, the kingdom of David will survive; the nations who oppose it are about to be defeated.

As I mentioned above, within the book of Isaiah the Immanuel prophecy seems to be connected to King Ahaz's son, King Hezekiah. Among other things, the prophet later uses the expression "your land, O Immanuel" (Isaiah 8:8). This makes it sound like the land belongs in some way to Immanuel. This way of speaking fits the idea that Immanuel is the future royal ruler. Later Jewish sources therefore explicitly connect the Immanuel passage with Hezekiah.[1]

But if the oracle addresses a situation in the 700s B.C., how can Matthew say it is fulfilled in Jesus? Some argue that Matthew has misunderstood the passage in Isaiah. They claim it has nothing to do with Jesus' Virgin Birth. Notice that the word "virgin" never even appears in the translation of Isaiah's oracle given above. Why? In the original Hebrew, the mother of the Immanuel child is called an *'almah*, which means "young woman." There is another Hebrew word that more explicitly means "virgin," *bethulah*. Yet, as many have pointed out, Isaiah's Immanuel prophecy does not use the latter term.

Has Matthew made a mistake? To understand his use of Isaiah's oracle, we need to recognize that the Gospel writer interprets it in a *Jewish* way.

The Messiah as Emmanuel

To understand Matthew's use of Isaiah's prophecy, let us look at another oracle found in the book of Micah. There we hear about a coming ruler from Bethlehem:

---

1   See *Exodus Rabbah* 18:5; *Numbers Rabbah* 14:2; cf. also Justin Martyr, *Dialogue with Trypho* 43.8; 67.1; 77.1.

> But you, O Bethlehem Ephrathah, who are small among the
> regions of Judah, from you shall come forth for me one *who
> is to be ruler in Israel, whose origin is from of old, from ancient
> days.* Therefore he shall give them up until the time when she
> who is in travail gives birth. (Micah 5:2–3)

As we shall see later, this passage from Micah becomes important to the Christmas story. In the Gospel of Matthew, Jesus'
birth in Bethlehem is viewed as fulfilling Micah's prophecy
(Matthew 2:3–6).

For our purposes here, however, notice that Micah's oracle
has remarkable parallels with the Immanuel prophecy in Isaiah.

Oracle of Immanuel's Birth (Isaiah 7:14)	Oracle of the Future Ruler's Birth (Micah 5:3)
"Therefore, the Lord himself will give …"	"Therefore he shall give them …"
"… a young woman shall conceive and give birth"	"… she who is in travail gives birth"

It is hard to think that these similarities are merely coinci-
dental. In fact, scholars have argued that Micah's prophecy
about the future ruler from Bethlehem intentionally borrows
from Isaiah's Immanuel oracle.[2] In other words, Micah seems
to apply the passage in Isaiah to the notion of a coming ruler
from David's line. For what it is worth, later Jewish sources
explicitly interpret Micah's prophecy as referring to the Messiah.[3] All of this makes sense.

---

2   See, e.g., Hans Walter Wolff, *Micah: A Commentary*, trans. Gary Stansell (Minneapolis: Fortress, 1990), 145.

3   See Targum on Micah 5:2–3 and Targum Pseudo-Jonathan on Genesis 35:21. (A Targum
is an ancient translation of the Hebrew Bible into the Aramaic language.)

At its most fundamental level, Isaiah's Immanuel prophecy confirms God's promise to preserve the kingdom of David. Yet neither Hezekiah nor any other king in Israel's past achieved lasting peace. Isaiah's oracle could therefore be used in reference to a *future* ruler, a coming son of David par excellence. In that future king, the Immanuel prophecy would find its deepest meaning.

Matthew therefore naturally understands Jesus as the true "Emmanuel," the fulfillment of God's promises. Isaiah assures King Ahaz that the kingdom of David will be saved. In Christ, this is realized in its most profound sense: in him, David's kingdom is preserved forever.

Moreover, Matthew shows us that Jesus really is "Emmanuel"—he is "God with us." As in the Gospel of Luke, Jesus is identified in Matthew as "Lord, Lord" (Matthew 7:21; cf. Matthew 25:11). As we have seen, in the Greek version of the Old Testament the double use of "Lord, Lord" is used only for the God of Israel. In speaking of himself as "Lord, Lord," then, Jesus reveals his divine identity. Other indicators of Jesus' divinity in Matthew could also be highlighted. For example, at the end of the Gospel Jesus tells his disciples to go out to all nations and "[baptize] them in the name of the Father and of the Son and of the Holy Spirit" (Matthew 28:19). New Testament scholar John Meier writes:

> One could hardly imagine a more forceful proclamation of Christ's divinity—and, incidentally, of the Spirit's distinct personality—than this listing together, on a level of equality, of Father, Son, and Spirit. One does not baptize people in the name of a divine person, a holy creature, and an impersonal divine force.[4]

---

4   John P. Meier, *Matthew*, New Message 3 (Wilmington: Michael Glazier, 1980), 371–72.

In the end, then, Matthew shows that the promise of "God with us" is realized in its truest sense in Jesus. One need not insist that Isaiah's prophecy refers *either* to Hezekiah *or* to Jesus. The prophecy can refer to *both*—though, for Matthew, it has its most profound meaning in Christ.

Mary as Emmanuel's Virgin Mother

Yet if Jesus is truly "God with us," Matthew shows us that Isaiah's prophecy is fittingly applied to Jesus for another reason: the Emmanuel's mother is, astonishingly, an actual "virgin." While the Hebrew word *'almah* used in Isaiah's oracle does not *necessarily* mean virgin, it often includes that connotation. The word usually refers to a young, unmarried woman. For that reason, a woman described as an *'almah* is typically a virgin. For example, in Genesis, *'almah* is applied to Rebekah (Genesis 24:43), who, at the time, is also explicitly said to be a "virgin" (*bethulah*; Genesis 24:16). This explains the way Isaiah's prophecy was translated into the Greek version of the Old Testament. There the Hebrew word *'almah* is rendered with the Greek term *parthenos*, the standard word for "virgin." Isaiah's oracle, therefore, can be seen as having multiple fulfillments. It can refer to someone like Hezekiah, who was not the product of a virgin birth. But it is also realized in its fullest sense in Mary's conception of Jesus—she is the true virgin mother of "God with us."

But why is it so important that Mary is a "virgin" in the first place? As we have seen, her identity as virgin confirms that Jesus has no human father. He is the true Son of God, not by adoption, like the kings of the Old Testament, but by nature. The Virgin Birth reveals that while Jesus is fully human, he is also truly the Emmanuel, "God with us."

Finally, there is one last thing to say about Jesus' fulfillment of Isaiah's prophecy. If the Immanuel child refers to a future king, which seems likely, this has an important consequence for the identity of the child's mother. In the kingdom of David, the *mother* of the king often served as queen (2 Kings 10:13; Jeremiah 29:2).[5] For example, the Bible recounts how King Solomon, David's son, treated his mother, Bathsheba, as royalty:

> Bathsheba went to King Solomon to speak to him on behalf of Adonijah. And the king rose to meet her, and *he bowed down to her*. Then he sat on his throne, and had *a throne set up for the mother of the king*, and *she sat on his right*. Then she said, "I have one small request to make of you, do not refuse me." And the king said to her, "*Make your request, my mother, for I will not refuse you.*" (1 Kings 2:19–20)

Notice that the mother of the king is given a "throne" (Hebrew: *kissēʾ*) like Solomon's. In addition, we see that the queen mother makes requests of the king on behalf of others.

If the Immanuel child is a future king, the mother of Immanuel is likely the queen. Therefore, if Jesus is Emmanuel, this has implications for Mary—she would be the queen mother. In keeping with this line of thought, the woman presented as Jesus' mother in the book of Revelation is also said to wear a "crown" (Revelation 12:1). In addition, we can observe that Mary takes the needs of others to Jesus in the Gospel of John (John 2:3). As the queen mother brought requests to the son of David in the Old Testament, Mary intercedes on behalf of others, taking their needs to Jesus.

---

5   See the full study in Edward Sri, *Queen Mother: A Biblical Theology of Mary's Queenship* (Steubenville: Emmaus Academic, 2005).

To see Mary as the queen mother is not, therefore, somehow inappropriate. In no way does it detract from Jesus' identity as King. In fact, Jesus shares his dominion with others. For instance, as King Solomon had twelve officers over his kingdom (1 Kings 4:7), Jesus appoints the twelve apostles to judge the twelve tribes of Israel (Matthew 19:28; Luke 22:30). In this, Jesus fulfills hopes for the restoration of David's kingdom. To see Mary as queen mother fits well with this kind of fulfillment; as the king in the Old Testament had twelve officers and a queen mother, it is fitting that Jesus does as well.

Yet the significance of Mary's virginity is not simply due to Isaiah's Emmanuel prophecy. Although this oracle may be in the background of his Gospel, Luke, unlike Matthew, never quotes it. Here we will consider another reason Mary's virginity is fitting. But before we get to that, let us look at Mary's role as virgin in the Gospel of Luke.

Mary as Virgin

After Gabriel announces to Mary that she will be the mother of the Messiah, she responds with a question that begins: "How will this be?" (Luke 1:34). This seems like a strange reaction to the angel's news. Mary is betrothed. She will soon begin living with her husband. Why, then, would she find it surprising to learn that she will have a child?

"I Do Not Know Man"

The full question Mary poses to Gabriel is "How will this be since *I do not know man [andra ou ginōskō]*?" (Luke 1:34). To "know man" obviously refers to having sexual relations. At the simplest level, then, Mary is saying, "I do not have sexual relations." Yet her response seems to imply more than that.

When we look closely at Mary's question in the original Greek, it seems Mary is saying that she intends to *remain* a virgin. New Testament scholar Brant Pitre explains:

> Mary's words ... have the same force as the English words: "I do not smoke." Just as someone who says, "I do not smoke" means "I do not smoke (presently) nor do I have any intentions of smoking (in the future)," so too Mary's words mean "I do not have sexual relations (presently) nor do I intend to have relations (in the future)."[6]

Yet if Mary expects to remain a virgin, why is she betrothed?

Some have suggested that we should not read too much into Mary's question asking how she can conceive a son since she is a virgin. It is claimed that Luke only has Mary say this so that Gabriel has a reason to explain how Jesus will be born. Mary's question, it is claimed, therefore does not need to make sense. It only serves as a parallel to the scene with Zechariah, who also asks the angel a question when he hears the news that his wife will conceive (Luke 1:18: "How shall I know this? For I am an old man, and my wife is advanced in years"). This, however, is unconvincing. Luke is a skillful writer. He could have worded Mary's response differently. As New Testament scholar David Landry writes, "the story should make sense as a story to the reader."[7]

For his part, Landry insists that Mary assumes the angel means her pregnancy will begin immediately, that is, before she will live with Joseph. She is confused because she does

6   Brant Pitre, *Jesus and the Jewish Roots of Mary: Unveiling the Mother of the Messiah* (New York: Image, 2018), 106.

7   David T. Landry, "Narrative Logic in the Annunciation to Mary" (Luke 1:26–38)," *Journal of Biblical Literature* 114/1 (1995): 65–79.

not know how this can happen. Yet as other New Testament scholars observe, this is also unsatisfying. The angel has only told Mary that she *will* conceive sometime in the future, not that this is imminent.[8] In fact, Mary does not say, "I do not *yet* know man," but insists, "I do not know man," which, as we have seen, indicates she intends to refrain from sexual activity.

Ancient Christian writers in both the East and the West had another explanation for Mary's response: they believed that Mary's question only makes sense if she has taken some sort of sacred vow of virginity. This idea first appears in a book known as the *Protoevangelium of James*, which can be roughly dated to sometime in the late 100s.[9] The work contains many problems, including historical inaccuracies about the first-century Jewish world. Nonetheless, it shows us that the belief that Mary had taken some sort of vow of virginity was held by very early Christians.

But is it believable that Mary would have expected to remain a virgin after being betrothed to Joseph?

Sexual Abstinence in the Ancient Jewish World

New Testament scholar Raymond Brown writes, "In our knowledge of Palestinian Judaism, there is nothing that would explain why a twelve-year-old girl would have entered marriage with the intention to preserve virginity."[10] He argues that it is unlikely Mary would choose to be childless, since not having children was viewed as being in a state of disgrace (Luke 1:25).

---

8   John Nolland, *Luke,* 3 vols. (Dallas: Word Books, 1989), 1:52.

9   Bart Ehrman and Zlatko Pleše, *The Apocryphal Gospels* (Oxford: Oxford University Press, 2011), 31–35.

10   Raymond E. Brown, *The Birth of the Messiah: New Updated Edition* (New Haven, CT: Yale University Press, 1993), 304–5.

Yet, although Brown was a meticulous scholar, more recent work raises issues that undermine his position. For one thing, his insistence that childlessness was always seen as a sign of divine rejection should be questioned.[11] To maintain that no Jewish woman would refrain from having children due to concerns about being socially stigmatized is unconvincing.

More importantly, Brown's statement that "there is nothing that would explain" Mary's apparent intention to remain a virgin has also been shown to be inaccurate. Brant Pitre highlights evidence that indicates that at least some Jewish women *did* make such promises.[12] In the Torah, the most authoritative source for ancient Jewish life, we find laws that specifically deal with vows taken by women. In the book of Numbers, fathers and husbands are said to be able to invalidate such vows. This was not an obscure section of the law. It is cited in other Jewish sources.[13]

Regarding the vows taken by a wife, the Torah says:

Any vow and any binding oath to deny herself, her *husband* may allow to stand, or her husband may nullify. (Numbers 30:13)

What kind of vow is in view here? The passage talks about a vow through which a woman pledges to "deny herself" (*'annoth nephesh,* Numbers 30:13). As Pitre shows, though this term can refer to fasting, Old Testament scholars such as Jacob Milgrom have observed that *it also can refer to sexual abstinence.*[14] In context, this meaning makes the most sense.

---

11   Candida R. Moss and Joel S. Baden, *Reconceiving Infertility: Biblical Perspectives on Procreation and Childlessness* (Princeton, NJ: Princeton University Press, 2015).
12   For what follows, see the discussion and sources in Pitre, *Jesus and the Jewish Roots of Mary,* 108–12.
13   11QTemple (11Q19) 54:1–7; Philo, *Special Laws* 2.24; *Allegorical Interpretation* 2.63.
14   Jacob Milgrom, *Numbers,* The JPS Torah Commentary (Philadelphia: Jewish Publication Society, 1990), 246; Baruch Levine, *Numbers 21–36,* Anchor Bible 4A (New York: Doubleday, 2000), 433.

Ancient authors inform us that pledges of sexual abstinence were made by at least some Jews in the first century. This was a practice associated with the Essenes and the Therapeutae.[15] The Dead Sea Scrolls also indicate that married members of its community only had relations for the purpose of procreation; outside of that, having relations was viewed as sinful. This is likely the reason the Scrolls talk about "one who comes near to fornicate with his wife contrary to the Law."[16] To have sexual relations apart from procreation was, for these contemporaries of Mary, tantamount to fornication. Some will insist that these other Jewish groups have no bearing whatsoever on understanding Mary's outlook in Luke. That is not convincing. Though she was not a member of them, we see that sexual abstinence was prized by at least some of her Jewish contemporaries.

Finally, the Mishnah—a second-century collection that contains earlier Jewish traditions—indicates that married Jews would take vows of sexual abstinence, which could serve as grounds for divorce.[17] While such sources must be used cautiously, there is no reason to believe this lacks a historical basis. That Mary would have planned on practicing sexual abstinence after being married is therefore not as farfetched as some have made it out to be.

Jesus' "Brothers" and "Sisters"

Before moving on, we should mention passages that are cited as evidence that Mary did not remain a virgin.[18] Most

---

15 Josephus, *Jewish War* 2.160–61; Philo, *On the Contemplative Life* 68.

16 4Q270 7.i.12–13.

17 Mishnah Ketuboth 7:3–7.

18 For further sources and discussion, see the excellent study by James Prothro, "Semper Virgo? A Biblical Review of a Debated Dogma," *Pro Ecclesia* 28 (2019): 78–97.

famously, the New Testament speaks of Jesus having "brothers" and "sisters." For example, surprised by Jesus' ministry, the people in the Gospel of Mark ask:

> Is not this the carpenter, the son of Mary and *brother of James and Joses and Judas and Simon*? And are not *his sisters* here with us? (Mark 6:3; cf. Matthew 13:55–56)

Yet it is not as clear as some people make it out to be that Jesus' "brothers" and "sisters" are children of his mother. For one thing, the Greek nouns used for "brother" (Greek: *adelphos*) and "sister" (Greek: *adelphē*) can also refer to cousins or other relatives. To give just one example, in the Greek version of the Old Testament, Abraham refers to his *nephew* Lot as his "brother," using the same noun that is used for Jesus' relatives (Genesis 13:8: *adelphos*).

Moreover, none of the "brothers" or "sisters" of Jesus are ever said to be children of Jesus' mother. Some ancient writers believed that they were children of Joseph from a previous wife who had died. This seems unlikely, though. If we closely follow the way Mark's Gospel unfolds, we find good reason to think that Jesus' "brothers" and "sisters" are the children of a *different woman who is alive at Jesus' death*.

In Mark's account of Jesus' Crucifixion, we are told about women who witnessed Jesus' death:

> And there were also women looking from a distance, among whom were Mary Magdalene, and *Mary the mother of James the younger and of Joses*, and Salome, who when he was in Galilee, followed him, and ministered to him, and many other women who came up with him to Jerusalem. (Mark 15:40–41)

Who is the person named "Mary *the mother of James the younger and Joses*"? Mark simply identifies her by naming her sons, James and Joses. It seems he thinks the reader will recognize these brothers. But if so, who are they? What makes them so important? Have we already encountered them in the Gospel story? It seems that we have—James and Joses are said to be Jesus' "brothers" in the very passage we quoted above that speaks of Jesus' relatives (Mark 6:3). Significantly, the names "James" and "Joses" never appear together elsewhere in Mark. So, when Mark later tells us about a woman who is the mother of a "James" and a "Joses," *the most likely meaning is that these are the same men mentioned earlier.* James and Joses are therefore likely the sons of another Mary, not the mother of Jesus. If this woman is Jesus' mother, it makes no sense to refer to her as the mother of these brothers without mentioning Jesus. If Jesus was her son, the easiest way to clarify her identity would be to call her "Mary the mother of Jesus."[19] Therefore, James and Joses are probably not sons of Jesus' mother.

Corroborating evidence can be found in the Gospel of John. In his account of the Crucifixion of Jesus, we are told:

> But standing by the cross of Jesus were *his mother*, and *his mother's sister, Mary the wife of Clopas*, and Mary Magdalene. (John 19:25)

John confirms what Mark also says: there was *another* Mary at the foot of the Cross besides Mary the mother of Jesus (and Mary Magdalene): "Mary the wife of Clopas." Although it is possible that the reference to Jesus' "mother's sister" refers to a separate, unnamed person, this would be odd. Why name all the other women except this one? Because of this, it seems more likely that Jesus' "mother's sister" is "Mary the wife of

---

19 Joel Marcus, *Mark 8–16*, Anchor Yale Bible 27A (New Haven, CT: Yale University Press, 2009), 1060.

Clopas" (John 19:25). If this other Mary is both the mother of James and Joses *and* Jesus' "mother's sister," we have confirmation that James and Joses are Jesus' cousins. Furthermore, if James and Joses are not the sons of Jesus' mother, there is no reason to insist that his other "brothers" and "sisters" are her children. For these and other reasons, ancient Christian writers therefore conclude that these relatives are Jesus' *cousins*.[20]

Other Passages Relating to the Question of Mary's Virginity

People have pointed to other verses in the Gospels as "proof" that Mary had children after Jesus. In Matthew, for example, we read that Joseph took Mary as his wife but "knew her not *until* she gave birth to a son" (Matthew 1:25). This is sometimes said to be evidence that Mary had normal marital relations with Joseph after Jesus was born. Yet this over-reads the Greek. The ancient Bible scholar Jerome points out that the Greek word translated "until" (*heos*) does not necessarily refer to a change in circumstances. For example, Jesus tells the disciples that he will be with them "*until* [*heos*] the close of the age" (Matthew 28:20). It would be wrong to conclude that this means he will abandon them after the Second Coming. Likewise, the Greek translation of the Old Testament says that the daughter of King Saul "had no child *until* [*heos*] the day of her death" (2 Samuel 6:23). The word "until" (*heos*) does not imply that this situation changed after she died. It simply means what it says: she had no child *up to the time she died*. Therefore, when Matthew says Joseph had no relations with Mary "until" Jesus was born, he does not

---

20 See, e.g., Jerome, *Against Helvidius* 12.

necessarily imply this changed after the nativity. Matthew is simply making the point that Joseph cannot be Jesus' biological father. To read more into the verse than that is to go beyond its meaning.

Others point out that Jesus is called Mary's "firstborn" son in Luke (Luke 2:7). Yet this need not imply that she had other children. The expression refers to a child's legal status under the Mosaic law (Exodus 13:2; Numbers 3:12).

There is good reason to think, then, that Mary's question to the angel indicates that she expects to *remain* a virgin. The news that she will have a child is therefore astonishing. Yet God is fulfilling the hopes of Israel in spectacular ways—in ways no one could have anticipated. The birth of the Messiah to a virgin fits this pattern. But there is another reason why Mary's virginity is significant.

The New Creation

In the New Testament, virginity can be connected to the Jewish hope for *a new creation*. This is seen in various ways. Notably, we find this idea in both Gospels that emphasize Mary's virginity: Matthew and Luke.

Jewish Hopes for a New Creation

As we have discussed before, Jewish hopes for the future often involved the idea that God would bring about a new creation. For example, the Lord declares the following in the book of Isaiah:

> For behold, I create *new heavens, and a new earth*. (Isaiah 65:17)

Hopes for the renewal of the cosmos can be found in other ancient Jewish sources such as nonbiblical works like 1 Enoch and Jubilees (1 Enoch 45:1–5; 72:1; Jubilees 1:29; 4:26).

What we should emphasize here is that the expectation of a coming new creation was linked to hopes for the resurrection of the dead. For example, in 2 Maccabees a righteous mother courageously encourages her son to embrace martyrdom for the Jewish faith. In doing so, she explains that the Creator will one day raise him to new life:

> *The Creator of the world, who shaped the beginning of man and devised the origin of all things*, will in his mercy *give life and breath back to you again.* (2 Maccabees 7:23)

Just as God created the world, so too will he bring about a *new creation*, which will involve the resurrection of the righteous. The dead, then, will share in God's future renewal of the cosmos. In the New Testament, Jesus clearly affirms such hopes.

Virginity and the New Creation

Jewish new creation hopes are affirmed by Jesus in the Gospels. For example, in the Gospel of Matthew, Jesus speaks of a "new creation" (Greek: *palingenesia*, Matthew 19:28). He also affirms that the righteous will share in the new creation through the resurrection.

For our purposes, we should make a further observation: according to Jesus, the righteous who rise from the dead *will not marry*. Consider the following passage from the Gospel of Luke:

> The sons of this age marry and are given in marriage, but those who are deemed worthy to attain to that age and to the resurrection from the dead *neither marry nor are given in marriage.* (Luke 20:34–35)

According to Jesus, those who share in the new creation through the resurrection of the body will have a virgin-like status; they "neither marry nor are given in marriage." Jesus makes the same point in the Gospels of Matthew and Mark (Matthew 22:30; Mark 12:25).

Interestingly, the connection between virginity and the new creation can also be found in the writings of Paul. In 1 Corinthians, Paul encourages his readers not to marry: "He who marries his betrothed does well, and *he who refrains from marriage will do even better*" (1 Corinthians 7:38). To be sure, Paul is not denigrating marriage; he affirms that marriage is a divine "calling" (1 Corinthians 7:17). Nevertheless, Paul also believes that some should remain virgins. He says:

> The unmarried woman or virgin cares about the things of the Lord, that she may be holy both in body and in spirit: but she that is married cares for *the things of the world*, how she may please her husband. (1 Corinthians 7:34)

For the Apostle, married life belongs to *this world*—that is, to the old creation. Those who choose virginity, then, would seem to do so out of a renunciation of the "things that are of this world" (1 Corinthians 7:33).

Notably, Paul introduces his teaching about virginity with a statement about the transience of the present world:

> For the form of this world is passing away. (1 Corinthians 7:31)

Virginity, then, is a calling anchored in the recognition that the present form of the world is passing away. The implication is that virginity is connected to the hope of *a new world, a new creation*.

In light of the larger teaching of the New Testament, then, we can see why it is especially fitting that Mary is the *virgin* mother of Jesus. The Messiah ushers in the new creation. Paul says that those who are in Christ are a "new creation" (2 Corinthians 5:17). Since Mary is the mother of the Messiah, it is appropriate that she is known as the "Virgin Mary." This does not mean that all Christians are called to be virgins. It simply means that Mary symbolizes in her virginity the new creation that Jesus comes to inaugurate.

Mary as the New Eve

Finally, we should mention that the early Church Fathers saw great significance in the fact that the redemption of the world came through the Yes of a virgin. Ancient Christian writers concluded that when Adam and Eve sinned, they were still virgins. Why? Because Genesis tells us that Adam "knew" his wife *after* they were driven out of the Garden of Eden, which happened because of their disobedience to God (Genesis 4:1). Writing somewhere around A.D. 180, the early Christian bishop Irenaeus believed this had important implications for interpreting Mary's role in the Gospel of Luke.

Irenaeus points out that, unlike Matthew's Gospel, which only traces Jesus' human genealogy back to Abraham, Luke's list of Jesus' ancestors goes all the way back to Adam himself (Luke 3:23–38). Irenaeus argues that this is noteworthy. He begins by saying, "Adam became the beginning of those who die." He goes on to highlight how Mary reverses Eve's disobedience:

The knot of Eve's disobedience was loosed by the obedience of Mary. For *what the virgin Eve had bound fast through unbelief, this did the virgin Mary set free through faith.*[21]

---

21 Irenaeus, *Against Heresies* 3.22.4, in *The Ante-Nicene Fathers*, 9 vols., ed. Alexander Roberts and James Donaldson (Buffalo, NY: Christian Literature, 1885), 1:455 (hereafter cited as *Ante-Nicene Fathers*).

For Irenaeus, the Virgin Mary succeeds where the virgin Eve failed. With Adam, Eve ushers sin into the world. However, the Virgin Mary is faithful and so becomes the mother of the Redeemer. Since Paul speaks of Jesus as the New Adam (1 Corinthians 15:45; Romans 5:14), early Christian writers found it obvious to identify Mary as the New Eve.

All of this emphasizes a point made above: Mary's virginity is important because it signals the way the Messiah, her son, ushers in a new creation. At the dawn of time, Eve was called the "mother of all the living" (Genesis 3:20). Mary can be viewed as the "New Eve," the mother of all of those who live in Christ.

To return to a point made earlier, Christmas is a homecoming. Jesus not only reigns over a kingdom, but this kingdom is also a *family*. Not only does Mary share in her son's reign, but so do all believers. It is no wonder, then, that Jesus will later speak of those who accept his teaching as "sons of the kingdom" (Matthew 13:38). At Christmastime, we are reminded that, like Mary, we too are to be included in Christ's royal family. As "Silent Night" says, we gather "round" her as she is with Christ in the family of God, where "all is bright."

Yet Mary is not the only one who must adjust expectations because of Jesus' coming. The same is also true for Joseph. We now turn to examine his role in the Christmas story.

6

"What Child Is This?": Joseph and His Dilemma

The traditional Christmas hymn "What Child Is This?," written by William Chatterson Dix in 1865, opens with these words:

> What child is this, who, laid to rest
> On Mary's lap is sleeping?
> Whom angels greet with anthems sweet
> While shepherds watch are keeping?

Jesus' birth evokes wonder—he is a child unlike any infant ever born.

Although he is not mentioned in the hymn, I often imagine Joseph, Mary's husband, singing its opening lines. As he looked upon the face of the baby Jesus, I suspect he reflected on how he first learned of Mary's pregnancy. "What child is this?" was precisely the question Joseph pondered.

Joseph is easy to forget about. He quietly fades into the background. In fact, he never utters a single word in any of the Gospels. Still, Matthew makes clear that Joseph has a crucial role to play in Jesus' birth. Why is Joseph so important? And what does he teach us about the mystery at the heart of the Christmas celebration? This chapter addresses these questions.

The Royal Carpenter

We can begin with a simple question: What do we know about Joseph? Matthew tells us that he was known as a carpenter (Matthew 13:55). Yet, as the Gospel makes clear, there was much more to him than that.

Joseph's Royal Family

The Gospel of Matthew begins with Jesus' genealogy (Matthew 1:1–17). For people today, reading the long list of Jesus' ancestors might seem tedious. For Matthew's Jewish readers, however, the genealogy would have been extremely significant. In it, they would discover that the royal line of King David had been preserved. It was alive and well in *Joseph's* family.

Matthew begins with Abraham and then lists his descendants. Going on, Matthew lists the kings who came from David, including Solomon, Rehoboam, and Hezekiah. Matthew's genealogy, then, represents not just descendants of David but the *royal successors to the throne*.

How it was determined *who* was the rightful successor to David is unclear to us. Nevertheless, Matthew's genealogy assumes *that* there was such a line. On a human level, Jesus is the Messiah because of his genealogy. That is the whole point of the introduction to Matthew's Gospel; Jesus is the heir to the throne of David by means of his genealogy.

But let us be clear: according to Matthew, *Jesus has a royal genealogy because he is the legal son of Joseph.* For Matthew, it is Joseph's line that makes Jesus the "son of David." Of course, Matthew will later make the point that Joseph is not Jesus' biological father. This, however, does not threaten Jesus' royal identity. For ancient peoples, biological descent was not necessary for royal succession. For example, Caesar Augustus, the emperor at the time of Jesus' birth, had become emperor because he had been adopted by Julius Caesar. Subsequent emperors Tiberias, Caligula, and Nero were also all adopted sons of their predecessors. In antiquity, biological descent was not decisive for royalty. Instead, it was often an *adopted* son who was given the throne of his father.

It is worth mentioning here that Augustine emphasizes that Joseph's love for Jesus is magnified by Jesus' adopted status. In a work that dates to the year A.D. 418, he says, "Joseph achieved much more satisfactorily in spirit what another man desires to achieve in the flesh."[1] In sum, Jesus was not less of a son to Joseph because he was adopted.

Joseph the Carpenter

What does all of this mean for our understanding of Joseph? Matthew tells us later that the crowds, amazed by Jesus' ministry, ask:

> Where did this man get this wisdom and these mighty deeds?
> *Is not this the carpenter's son?* (Matthew 13:54–55)

Notice that Jesus is identified as *the carpenter's* son, a reference to Joseph. Strikingly, the crowd appears completely ignorant that Joseph himself was of royal descent. Jesus is thought to come from humble origins, not royalty. The reference to Joseph's occupation emphasizes Jesus' lowly social status.

The Greek noun translated "carpenter" is *tektōn*. The word can have a range of meanings, including "stone mason," "woodworker," and "silversmith." It can also refer to a

---

1   Augustine, *Sermon* 51.26, in *Sermons III on the New Testament*, trans. Edmund Hill, O.P. (Brooklyn: New City Press, 1991), 37.

"contractor" or "builder." Outside of the New Testament, the earliest Christian sources seem to interpret the word as referring to Joseph's job as a "woodworker." Particularly noteworthy is Justin Martyr's statement that Jesus "used to work as a carpenter, making ploughs and yokes."[2] As one well-respected commentary on Matthew says, "We are probably to follow the Greek Fathers in thinking of Jesus as the son of a carpenter."[3]

Whatever the precise meaning of *tektōn,* it is indisputable that Joseph was not a wealthy man. The Holy Family's poverty is especially emphasized in Luke. After Jesus' birth, Joseph and Mary offer two turtle doves as a sacrifice in the temple (Luke 2:24). This was the offering prescribed for the poor (Leviticus 12:8).

Joseph, then, was a laborer. The book of Sirach talks about how such people did not have the leisure needed for study: "Every *carpenter* [*tektōn*] and master builder *labors by night just as by day* (Sirach 38:27). The crowds are therefore amazed at Jesus' ministry; carpenters were not expected to be teachers well-versed in the Scriptures.

It would hardly seem fitting for a royal heir to the throne to spend his life engaged in an occupation known as involving endless toil. Yet one should not be surprised that Joseph lived in obscurity. As we have mentioned, Herod was ruthless. He had his own wife and sons murdered out of fear that they might threaten his possession of the crown. Later, Matthew will recount how, in an attempt to murder the infant Jesus, whom the magi have come proclaiming as "king of the Jews" (Matthew 2:2), Herod massacres children in Bethlehem (Matthew 2:16). It is hardly any wonder, then, that Matthew indicates that Joseph's royal connections were apparently kept quiet.

---

2   Justin Martyr, *Dialogue with Trypho* 88, trans. Thomas B. Falls, in *The Writings of Justin Martyr* (Washington, DC: Catholic University of America Press, 1948), 290.

3   W.D. Davies and Dale C. Allison Jr., *The Gospel according to Saint Matthew,* 3 vols. (London: T&T Clark International, 2004), 2:456.

Yet his royal ancestry is not something Joseph apparently thinks about much in Matthew. What Matthew does talk about, however, is Joseph's response to the news of Mary's pregnancy. We now turn to consider this aspect of the Christmas story.

Joseph's Response to Mary's Pregnancy

Matthew tells us:

> Now the birth of Jesus Christ happened in this way: When his mother Mary was betrothed to Joseph, before they came together, she was found to be with child by the Holy Spirit. Then Joseph her husband, being a righteous man, and not willing to publicly shame her, decided to divorce her secretly. (Matthew 1:18–19)

Joseph knows that the child Mary is carrying is not his biological offspring. Matthew explicitly tells us that the couple had not had marital relations (Matthew 1:25). At this point in the narrative, they are "betrothed." But what was "betrothal"? And what are we to make of Joseph's response to the news of Mary's pregnancy?

First-Century Jewish Marriage Practices

To begin with, we should explain that betrothal was not the ancient equivalent of an "engagement" period. Couples who were betrothed were legally "husband" and "wife" (Deuteronomy 20:7; 28:30; Judges 14:15). While it is popular for preachers nowadays to describe Mary as an "unwed mother," that label is inaccurate. Joseph and Mary were married by law.

Nevertheless, during the betrothal period, virgin brides lived with their parents. This would last up to a year.[4]

Since they are married, Joseph's only way to terminate his relationship with Mary legally is through a divorce. It is true that the verb that is translated "divorce" (Greek: *apolysai*) can also mean "send away." Because of this, some have argued that Joseph did not actually contemplate getting a legal divorce but merely planned on sending Mary away quietly. This is unconvincing. When the verb Matthew uses appears within the context of ending a marital relationship, it refers to "divorce." If Matthew meant something else by it, he would have to specify this. In fact, when Matthew says Joseph decided to "*divorce [apolysai]* her secretly," he uses the same term that appears later when Jesus issues his startling teaching on divorce and remarriage (Matthew 5:31; 19:3, 7–9). The word means "divorce" there, just as it does here.

Interpretations of Joseph's Decision

But *why* did Joseph consider divorcing Mary? Over the centuries, three explanations have commonly been given. All three have been advanced by Fathers and Doctors of the Church.

1. Joseph Suspects Mary of Adultery. The view that easily remains the most popular with contemporary scholars is that Joseph seeks to divorce Mary because he suspects she has committed adultery. This way of reading the story is also attested in early sources. For example, in the *Protoevangelium of James*, Joseph compares Mary to Eve, accusing her of being seduced by the evil one. He pointedly asks her: "Why have you done this and forgotten the Lord your God?"[5] Likewise, writing

---

4   Mishnah Ketuboth 5:2; Mishnah Nedarim 10:5.

5   *Protoevangelium of James* 13:2, in *The Apocryphal New Testament*, ed. J. K. Elliot (Oxford: Oxford University Press, 1993).

sometime between A.D. 155 and 167, Justin Martyr says that Joseph wanted to divorce Mary "because he thought she was pregnant through human intercourse, namely, fornication."[6] Doctors of the Church such as John Chrysostom and Augustine take this view as well.[7] Advocates of this interpretation often claim that Joseph is said to be "righteous" because he protects Mary from stoning, the punishment the law assigns to adultery (Deuteronomy 22:13–29).

2. Joseph Fears to Live with Mary Out of Reverence for Her. Rather than holding that Joseph believes Mary committed adultery, some offer a radically different interpretation: Joseph decides to separate from Mary precisely because he knows her child is from God. Matthew says that Mary was "found to be with child *of the Holy Spirit*" (Matthew 1:18). The claim is made that this refers to Joseph—*he* discovered that Mary was "with child of the Holy Spirit." Yet, because of his humility, Joseph feared to live with Mary because he believed he was unworthy to live with this miraculous child and his mother. This is said to explain why the angel says, "Do not *fear* to take Mary as your wife" (Matthew 1:20). This view is advanced by Doctors of the Church such as Thomas Aquinas as well as modern writers such as the theologian Karl Rahner and the Bible scholar Ignace de la Potterie.[8]

3. Joseph Is Perplexed. The third interpretation might be seen as steering a middle path between the two discussed above. Its most prominent advocate is the Doctor of the Church Jerome. In this view, Joseph decides to divorce Mary because he was "perplexed by what had taken place."[9] This

---

6   Justin Martyr, *Dialogue with Trypho* 78, trans. Thomas B. Falls (Washington, DC: Catholic University of America Press, 2003), 272.

7   Augustine, *Sermon* 51.10; Chrysostom, *Homilies in Matthew* 4.7.

8   Aquinas, *Summa Theologiae* III, q. 29, art. 3, obj. 3; Karl Rahner, S.J., "Nimm das Kind und seine Mutter," *Geist und Leben* 30 (1957): 14–22; Ignace de la Potterie, S.J., *Mary in the Mystery of the Covenant* (New York: Alba House, 1992).

9   Jerome, *Commentary on Matthew* at Matthew 1:19, trans. Thomas P. Scheck (Washington, DC: Catholic University of America Press, 2008), 63.

view is also attested in the *Protoevangelium of James*. As I have mentioned above, according to this work Joseph first accuses Mary of committing adultery. In the story, however, Mary insists that she has no idea how she has become pregnant. She is portrayed—most improbably!—as having completely forgotten about the angel's announcement that she would give birth to the Son of God. Because Mary swears an oath, Joseph winds up uncertain of her infidelity. He worries that if she is innocent, he might be guilty of "delivering innocent blood to the judgement of death."[10] He even considers the possibility that the child may somehow be of supernatural origin. Perhaps, then, Joseph decides to divorce Mary because he concludes that since whatever is happening with Mary clearly does not involve him, he ought not involve himself with her any further. He does not want to be implicated in something that is not from God.

So, which interpretation of Joseph's response is most likely?

Weighing the Options

Most contemporary scholars agree that Joseph is not considering divorce because he fears to live with Mary. Matthew later relates that Joseph discovered how the child was conceived in a dream. An angel informs him: "Do not fear to take Mary as your wife *for that which is begotten in her is by the Holy Spirit*" (Matthew 1:20). To read the angel's statement as implying that Joseph already knows the child is from the Spirit misconstrues the Greek. In the angel's announcement to Joseph, the word "for" (*gar*) is introducing new information to Joseph. Consider the other angelic messages Joseph later receives in the Gospel:

---

10 *Protoevangelium of James* 14:2.

> Rise, take the child and his mother, and flee to Egypt, and remain there till I tell you; *for* [*gar*] Herod is about to search for the child, to destroy him. (Matthew 2:13)

> Rise, take the child and his mother, and go to the land of Israel, *for* [*gar*] those who sought the child's life are dead. (Matthew 2:20)

In each of the two instances, the word "for" (Greek: *gar*) announces something to Joseph that he *does not already know*. The same is true in the first instance. Joseph, therefore, does not know for certain how the child was conceived until the angel comes to him.

Nevertheless, the theory that Joseph believes Mary committed adultery is also not without problems. The supposition that Matthew portrays Joseph as "righteous" because he seeks to spare Mary from the legal consequences of adultery should also be questioned. This interpretation ignores that "righteousness" in the Gospel of Matthew refers to keeping the law. Jesus says, "Whoever therefore looses *one of the least of these commandments*, and teaches men thus, shall be called the least in the kingdom of heaven" (Matthew 5:19). To believe that Matthew calls Joseph "righteous" because he "relaxes" the law is a hard sell.

Where does the discussion above leave us? Joseph's plan to divorce Mary "privately" is indeed very strange. The fact is, we are never told what conclusion Joseph comes to about what has happened to Mary. The simplest explanation would seem to be that Joseph concludes that since the pregnancy does not involve him, it is best for him to separate from Mary. Whether he concludes Mary had sinned or not is simply never stated by Matthew. For these reasons, I lean toward Jerome's explanation.

What matters most of all, however, is that once Joseph hears the word of the Lord through the angel, he acts. Joseph responds in faith. This is worth considering more closely.

Joseph's Example of Faith

To all appearances, it may have seemed that God had bestowed a gift upon Joseph, royal lineage, that had no purpose. The line of David had been miraculously preserved through the centuries, but for what? Joseph, who came from kings, lives humbly as a carpenter. Joseph later discovers that his wife is mysteriously pregnant. None of the pieces of Joseph's life seem to fit together—until the angel speaks: in Christ, the puzzle of his life is solved. God's plan is that *Joseph* will be the one to give the Messiah his name, an act performed by a child's father (see Luke 1:62–63). In all of this, we see that Joseph is a model of faithfulness.

Joseph's Chastity

We should say something here about Joseph's age. Christian art often depicts him as significantly older than Mary. Yet we should probably doubt this portrait.

One reason Joseph is often thought to be elderly at the time of his betrothal to Mary is that he is not present in later scenes that mention Jesus' relatives (Matthew 12:46; Mark 3:31; Luke 8:19; John 2:12). That Joseph passed away by this point therefore seems likely. Nevertheless, this does not mean Joseph is an old man at the time of Jesus' birth. Noticeably, while Luke explicitly identifies Zechariah as an "old man" (*presbytēs*, Luke 1:18), the Gospels simply call Joseph a "man" (*anēr*, Luke 1:27; Matthew 1:19). If Joseph had been significantly older than Mary, one would expect the Gospel writers to mention this.

Joseph is also often depicted as elderly because artists were influenced by nonbiblical stories about the Holy Family found in works such as the *Protoevangelium of James*. These sources, which are of suspect historical value, often stress Joseph's advanced age for two reasons. First, some interpreters thought that the "brothers" and "sisters" of Jesus were children of Joseph from a previous marriage. Joseph was therefore portrayed as older since he had already been married. As we have seen, however, two of Jesus' "brothers" are said to be children of a woman who is alive at Jesus' death. They are, therefore, more likely to be Jesus' cousins.

Finally, Joseph is sometimes portrayed as elderly to account for his chaste relationship with Mary. In this, Joseph's abstinence is attributed to his advanced age rather than to his virtue. This, however, is unnecessary. If Mary had taken a vow like those described in the book of Numbers, Joseph would have had to approve it. Today it is often simply accepted that men are powerless over their carnal impulses. In the righteous Joseph, however, a very different portrait of what it means to be a man may be found.

Joining Joseph in the Dark

In the Old Testament, we read about a Joseph who learns of the divine plan through dreams (Genesis 37:5–11). The same is true of Joseph in the New Testament. The angel tells him,

> Joseph, son of David, do not fear to take Mary as your wife for that which is begotten in her is by the Holy Spirit. And she shall bear a son, and *you shall call his name Jesus*, for he shall save his people from their sins. (Matthew 1:20–21)

As "son of David" it will be *Joseph* who names the child Jesus, just as Zechariah names John the Baptist (Luke 1:57–63). In so doing, Joseph will become Jesus' father. In this, the Scriptures are fulfilled: the Messiah, the one who will bring "salvation," is the "son of David." Joseph, who works as a lowly carpenter, is the one God chooses to play a pivotal role in all of this. He who is powerless in the eyes of the world—a lowly and poor carpenter—is the very one responsible for the Messiah's identity as "son of David." With the coming of "God with us," the promise of Joseph's royal inheritance is finally realized.

In a work written sometime in the 300s, the Syriac writer Ephrem poignantly sums up Joseph's situation. He imagines Joseph saying the following prayer:

> I did not know that in [Mary's] womb was a great treasure
> that would suddenly enrich my poverty. David my forefather
> bore a diadem; but I, thrown down from that honor, have
> come upon utmost contempt; and him whom lineage des-
> tined to be a king, chance has made a carpenter. But now
> the crown that was snatched away has returned after you, the
> King of kings, has come into my arms.[11]

At Christmas, we would do well to reflect on what happened to Joseph.

Joseph was in the dark about the nature of Mary's pregnancy. Yet as soon as the angel comes to him and informs him of what has happened, he responds in faith. Becoming the adopted father of the Messiah would certainly not be a safe thing to do. When Herod discovers that the Christ has been born, he predictably targets him for destruction. Joseph does not, however, shrink back in fear. He ends up serving as the Holy Family's protector by listening to the directions he receives from the angel.

Joseph gives us an example to imitate. Like him, we can find ourselves placed in situations that make no sense.

---

11 Ephrem, *Hymns on the Nativity* 5.17–18. Translation of line 17 from Kathleen E. McVey, *Ephrem the Syrian: Hymns* (New York: Paulist Press 1989), 108. Translation of line 18 is modified from Francis L. Filas, S.J., *Joseph* (Boston: Daughters of St. Paul, 1962), 175–76.

Nevertheless, like Joseph, we are called to trust in the Lord and remain "righteous." In Christ, the puzzles in our lives find their resolution. This is true even if we do not always understand how that resolution can be realized.

In addition, what Joseph shows us is that worldly power and status are not the route to human fulfillment. The greatest gifts of God are not recognized by the world. At Christmastime, when the dangers of commercialism are especially high, this is a timely reminder. Joseph toils in obscurity. The King of Kings is laid in a manger. Our next chapter focuses on the significance of this aspect of the Christmas story.

7

"Away in a Manger": Jesus' Birth in Bethlehem

The classic hymn "Away in a Manger," which some have incorrectly attributed to the Protestant Reformer Martin Luther, offers an iconic description of Jesus' birth:

> Away in a manger
> No crib for a bed
> The little Lord Jesus
> Laid down His sweet head.

As we shall see, the detail that Jesus was laid in a manger is taken from the Gospel of Luke. The song goes on to portray the Christ child as "asleep on the hay." The lyrics paint a familiar picture: Jesus is placed among animals.

Yet, although manger scenes frequently include an ox and donkey, the Gospels never mention their presence in the place where Jesus is born. Where do we get such imagery? Why do *these* animals show up so frequently in nativity scenes?

This chapter looks more carefully at the story of Jesus' birth in Luke and the way it has been interpreted in Christian tradition. Why is it significant that Jesus is born in Bethlehem? Why do Bible translations say that there was no "room" for the Holy Family in the "inn"? Was there some sort of "Hotel

Bethlehem" with a "No Vacancy" sign in the window? Finally, why does Luke mention that Jesus was laid in a "manger"? This chapter looks at all these questions. We begin with the significance of Bethlehem itself.

The Little Town of Bethlehem

Both Matthew and Luke tell us that Jesus was born in Bethlehem. At first, the mention of this city may seem like a minor detail. Yet Jesus' birth in this town is profoundly meaningful.

The Birthplace of the Messiah

Bethlehem was not a powerful city. To the contrary, it seems to have been viewed as a relatively insignificant place. What made the village noteworthy was its role in Israel's past; it was the birthplace of the greatest king in Israel's history: David. Moreover, as we saw in a previous chapter, the prophet Micah announces that the future ruler of Israel will come from here. Matthew explicitly quotes this prophecy.

When the magi come looking for the infant king, Herod assembles all the Jewish scribes to learn where the Messiah will be born. Citing Micah's prophecy, the Scripture experts tell him that the Messiah will be born in Bethlehem:

> And gathering together all the chief priests and scribes of the people, he inquired from them where the Christ was to be born. Then they said to him, "In Bethlehem of Judaea, for thus it is written by the prophet, 'And you Bethlehem of the land of Judah are by no means least among the rulers of Judah: for from you shall go forth a ruler who shall

shepherd my people Israel.'" (Matthew 2:4–6, citing Micah 5:2; cf. 2 Samuel 5:2)

Jesus, the Messiah, is born right where he should be.

Jesus' Birth in God's Plan

In Luke, Jesus' birth takes place in Bethlehem because the Holy Family must go there to comply with an imperial edict.

> Now it happened in those days that a decree went out from Caesar Augustus that all the world should be enrolled. This was the first enrollment when Quirinius was governor of Syria. And all went to be enrolled, each one to his own city. And Joseph also went up from Galilee, out of the city of Nazareth, to Judea, to the city of David, which is called Bethlehem because he was of the house and lineage of David, to be enrolled with Mary, his betrothed, who was with child. And it happened that while they were there, the time came for her to give birth. (Luke 2:1–6)

A discussion of how Luke's chronological details relate to what is known from other sources is not possible here. What Luke's presentation highlights is this: the powers that be think they are calling the shots, but God's plan will ultimately be accomplished. Jesus is born in the king's hometown, as is fitting. The pagan emperor issues his decrees for his purposes. Unbeknownst to him, however, God uses them to make sure the Messiah is born in the right place. In other words, even if the world does not know it, the Lord is the real King. The true home of the King is not the splendid city of Rome, capital of the empire; it is the "Little Town of Bethlehem."

In addition, the humble circumstances of Jesus' birth are emphasized in another way—he is laid unceremoniously in a manger. But what does the manger signify?

The Manger Scene

In 1223, Francis of Assisi decided to mark the feast of Christ's birth in a new way. Wanting to emphasize the poverty of Jesus, Francis placed a statue of Christ in a manger with hay. An ox and a donkey were also included in the scene. With this, Francis began the tradition of erecting a Christmas crèche, that is, a depiction of Christ's nativity. As one historian says of the Francis story, "There is no reason to doubt the historicity of the crèche."[1] Francis' idea soon gained popularity. Manger sets are now commonplace at Christmastime. Yet if we look closely at the Gospels, we find no mention of certain features they often include. They say nothing about the presence of an ox and donkey at Jesus' birth. Why, then, did Francis include them?

Archaeology and Jesus' Birthplace

In Luke, we read: "And [Mary] gave birth to her firstborn son and wrapped him in swaddling clothes." (Luke 2:7). Here Mary is depicted as tenderly caring for the infant Jesus. Swaddling an infant was common practice; even the great Solomon was swaddled as a babe (Wisdom 7:4). A child who was not

---

1   Augustine Thompson, O.P., *Francis of Assisi: A New Biography* (Ithaca, NY: Cornell University Press, 2012), 260; also 108–9.

swaddled could even be viewed as a victim of parental aban-
donment (cf. Ezekiel 16:4).

What Luke goes on to say has often been misunderstood.
For example, an influential English Bible, the King James
Version, puts it this way: "And [Mary] laid him in a manger;
because there was no room for them in the inn" (Luke 2:7).
This reading gives the impression that Mary and Joseph
were wandering around Bethlehem looking for a hotel only
to discover no available rooms. This reading is reinforced by
various film adaptations of the Gospel story. In these, Joseph
and Mary are portrayed as being sent out into the night by
a heartless innkeeper before finding refuge in a stable, where
Mary gives birth.

Various Christian practices have emerged out of the
understanding that Mary and Joseph looked in vain for a
place to stay in Bethlehem. For example, by the 1800s, the
Irish placed candles in their windows to signify their desire
to welcome Christ into their homes. According to Joseph
Kelly, the custom of decorating homes with Christmas lights
can be traced back to this custom.[2] Similarly, the Mexican
tradition of *Las Posadas* reenacts Mary and Joseph's search
for accommodations. This devotional is a beautiful reminder
of the need to embrace the poor, in whom Christ comes
to us.

Yet the idea that the Holy Family was unable to find a place
to stay and therefore had to make do with a stable is not found
in the actual Gospel story. For one thing, Luke never mentions an "inn."[3] The Greek word that the King James Version

---

2   Joseph F. Kelly, *The Feast of Christmas* (Collegeville, MN: Liturgical Press, 2010), 100.

3   For the following, see Benjamin A. Foreman, "Luke's Birth Narrative," in *Lexham Geo-
graphic Commentary on the Gospels*, ed. Barry J. Beitzel (Bellingham: Lexham Press, 2017),
10–18; Stephen Carlson, "The Accommodations of Joseph and Mary in Bethlehem," *New
Testament Studies* 56 (2010): 326–42.

renders as "inn" is *katalyma*. Later, Luke uses the term to refer to a guest room (Luke 22:11). When Luke wants to refer to an "inn," he uses a different Greek term: *pandocheion* (Luke 10:34).

We should also note that Luke tells us that Mary and Joseph have apparently already been staying in Bethlehem when the time comes for Mary to have her baby. Luke tells us: "It happened that *while they were there*, the time came for her to give birth" (Luke 2:6). Contrary to various depictions, the nativity of Jesus does not take place on the night the couple arrives at the city.

How, then, are we to understand the scene depicted by Luke?

The Greek word the King James Version translates "room," *topos*, simply means "place" or even "space" (Luke 14:22). The idea in Luke, therefore, is that when Mary was about to give birth, the "place" where they were staying was not large enough to accommodate their needs. The best translation of the passage would simply be "there was no *space* [*topos*] for them in the *room* [*katalyma*]."

So where is the Holy Family staying if not in a hotel? Given ancient practices, the Holy Family would be expected to stay with relatives. Yet when it came time for Mary to deliver Jesus, the place where they were staying was too small to accommodate a birth. Notice that Luke does not just say that there was no space for a "child," but that there was no space for "*them* in the room." Besides Joseph, Mary likely would have been assisted by others, such as a midwife. It is worth pointing out that when the shepherds come later to report that angels had appeared to them, Luke says, "*All who heard it* were amazed" (Luke 2:18). This might imply that there were others besides Mary and Joseph with the child. Either way, the key point is that Jesus, the Messiah, is born in humble circumstances. The devotional instincts that underlie traditions like *Las Posadas* are beautiful and fitting; the Messiah was welcomed by only a few.

The Ox and the Donkey

Many have the impression that Jesus is born in some sort of stable—that is, an outside structure designed solely for animals. Most nativity scenes portray such a setting. Luke, however, never says this. It is important to read the Gospel story carefully.

As we have seen, Luke reports that Mary places the baby Jesus "in the *manger* because there was no *space* [*topos*] for them in the *room* [*katalyma*]" (Luke 2:7). The word translated "manger," *phatnē*, could refer to something like a "stall." Yet since we are told that the baby Jesus is swaddled before being placed in the *phatnē*, the word more likely refers to something like a feeding box or a trough—that is, a "manger."[4]

The manger is also probably not located outside. Simple first-century Jewish homes would ordinarily involve a dirt floor with two rooms: (1) a main room where the entire family ate meals, cooked, and slept together, and (2) a private chamber for guests. The living space of the main room would be slightly elevated. The place near the door in the main room would be used to house the family's domestic animals at night. Mangers would be placed there.[5] Keeping the animals in at night was desirable for two reasons. For one thing, animals heated up the house. For another, animals could be expensive; keeping them in the house at night protected them from theft.

---

4   Raymond E. Brown, *The Birth of the Messiah: New Updated Edition* (New Haven, CT: Yale University Press, 1993), 399.
5   See David A. Fiensy, "The Galilean House in the Late Second Temple and Mishnaic Periods," in *Galilee in the Late Second Temple and Mishnaic Periods*, vol. 1, *Life, Culture, and Society*, ed. David A. Fiensy and James Riley Strange (Minneapolis: Fortress, 2014), 216–41, esp. 229.

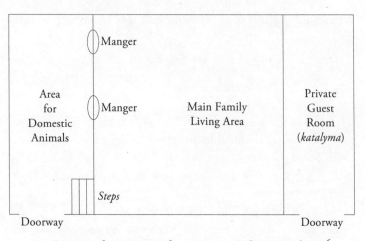

Layout of a common first-century Palestinian home[6]

But why did Francis include an ox and a donkey in his nativity scene? In the Greek version of the Old Testament, we read the following in the first chapter of Isaiah:

> The ox knows its owner, and the donkey knows the *manger* [*phatnē*] of its *lord* [*kyrios*], but Israel has not known me. (Isaiah 1:3)

Ancient Christian writers connected this passage with Luke's account, where the "Lord" (*kyrios*; cf. Luke 1:43) is laid in a "manger" (*phatnē*, cf. Luke 2:7, 12, 16). Reading the Old Testament in light of the New, they believed Isaiah's prophecy about the ox and the donkey pointed forward to Christ's birth. For example, in a homily dated between A.D. 394 and 413, Jerome says, "Why in a manger? That the prophecy of Isaiah the prophet might be fulfilled."[7]

---

6   Figure adapted from Kenneth Bailey, *Jesus through Middle Eastern Eyes* (Downers Grove, IL: InterVarsity Press, 2008), 33.

7   Jerome, *Homily* 88, trans. Sr. Marie Ligouri Ewald, in *The Homilies of Saint Jerome (Homilies 60–96)* (Washington, DC: Catholic University of America Press, 1966), 221.

The Cave in Bethlehem

Before moving on, it is worth noting that ancient Christian art often sets the nativity of Jesus in a cave. The biblical Gospels make no mention of such a setting. Nevertheless, the tradition that Jesus was born in a cave is attested in Justin Martyr's writings and in the *Protoevangelium of James*.[8] Whether one of these sources is dependent on the other is debated. Either way, since both these sources date to somewhere between A.D. 150 and 200, the cave tradition is rather early.

Writing in the mid-200s, the early Christian writer Origen seems to indicate that the cave where Mary gave birth to Jesus was known in his day: "There is shown at Bethlehem the cave where he was born, and the manger in the cave where he was wrapped in swaddling-clothes."[9] Later, between A.D. 312 and 318, the Christian historian Eusebius writes: "Now all agree that Jesus Christ was born in Bethlehem, and a cave is shown there by the inhabitants to those who come from abroad to see it."[10] How could the early Christians preserve the memory of such a site? Jerome tells us that they got help from Rome.

It seems that the Romans had the practice of erecting pagan shrines in places formerly revered by Jews and Christians. Most famously, the emperor Hadrian, who reigned from A.D. 117 to 138, is said to have erected a temple to the god Jupiter in Jerusalem, the previous location of the Jewish temple.[11] According to Jerome, Hadrian also transformed the place of Jesus' nativity into a pagan place of worship. Later, the emperor Constantine built a church over the spot.[12] The

---

8 Justin Martyr, *Dialogue with Trypho* 78.5; *Protoevangelium of James* 17:1—18:1.
9 Origen, *Against Celsus* 1.51, in *Ante-Nicene Fathers*, 4:418.
10 Eusebius, *Demonstration of the Gospel* 3.2, trans. W. J. Ferrar (New York: Macmillan, 1920).
11 Cassius Dio, *Roman History* 69.12.1. See also Schlomit Weksler-Bdolah, *Aelia Capitolina* (Leiden: Brill, 2019), 117–18.
12 Jerome, *Epistle to Paulinus* 58.3; cf. Eusebius, *Life of Constantine* 3.41.

Church of the Nativity, which stands in Bethlehem today, is likely built over the site of the original church.[13]

If Jesus was born in a cave, it would not change what we have said above. Kenneth Bailey, an expert on ancient Middle Eastern culture, observes that "many peasant homes in Palestine in the past were or began as caves."[14] Animals would be kept at night near the entry place for security and heat. Whatever one makes of the cave tradition, then, the imagery still holds—Jesus is placed where one would expect to find food. But why is this important?

The Manger and the Bread of Life

According to early Christian writers, the fact that the child Jesus is placed where food belongs is significant. For them, the manger is a symbol of the Church's eucharistic celebration. In this, the nativity story is inseparably connected to a concept at the heart of Christmas itself, "Christ's Mass."

The Manger and the Upper Room

As mentioned above, Luke says that Jesus is laid in a "manger" because there was no space in the "room." The Greek word translated "room," *kalalyma*, appears later in Luke's narrative. Notably, it is the noun used to describe the place where Jesus eats his Last Supper. When the disciples ask him where he will celebrate the Passover, he tells them where to go:

---

13 See Jordan J. Ryan, *From the Passion to the Holy Sepulchre* (London: T&T Clark, 2019), 135–81.

14 Kenneth E. Bailey, "The Manger and the Inn: The Cultural Background of Luke 2:7," *Theological Review* 2, no. 2 (1979): 33–44.

"Behold, when you have entered into the city, you will meet a man carrying a water jar. Follow him into the house in which he enters. And you shall say to the master of the house, 'The Teacher says to you: Where is the *guest room* [*katalyma*] where I may eat the Passover with my disciples?' And he shall show you a large upper room that is furnished: there prepare." And they went and found everything as he had said to them: and they prepared the Passover. (Luke 22:10–13)

Jesus eats the Last Supper, then, in a *katalyma,* the same word used in Luke's story of Jesus' birth.

By using the term *katalyma* in the story of Jesus' birth, Luke anticipates what will happen later in his Gospel. At his nativity, Jesus is placed in the "manger" because there is no space in the "room" (*katalyma*). Given what happens at the Last Supper, this cannot be unintentional. In the upper "room," Jesus explicitly identifies himself with bread. We read:

And he took bread, and after giving thanks, he broke it, and gave it to them, saying, "*This is my body* which is given for you: do this in remembrance of me." (Luke 22:19)

The one who is placed in the feeding trough later gives himself to the disciples as food.

Bethlehem as "House of Bread"

Ancient Christian writers believed that the manger points to the Eucharist. Cyril of Alexandria, who died in A.D. 444, writes:

Whereas we were brutish in soul, by now approaching the
manger, yes, his table, we find no longer feed, but the bread
from heaven, which is the body of life.[15]

Likewise, in a series of homilies delivered in the late 300s,
John Chrysostom says:

This body, even lying in a manger, magi reverenced. Let us,
then, at least imitate those Barbarians, we who are citizens
of heaven.... For they ... drew near with great awe; but you
behold him not in the manger but on the altar, not a woman
holding him in her arms, but the priest standing by.[16]

These Church Doctors explain that in the manger the bread
of life is present, and, likewise, in the Eucharist we come anew
to the manger.

Moreover, in connection with this eucharistic interpretation of the manger, early Christians observe that "Bethlehem"
means "house of bread" in Hebrew. Writing sometime in A.D.
230–240, Origen says: "Where else would the shepherds has-
ten after the message of peace than to the spiritual house of
the heavenly bread, Christ, i.e., the church."[17] Likewise, in a
homily that dates between A.D. 394 and 413, Jerome puts it
this way:

The fruit of our earth is the bread of life, who was born for us
at Bethlehem. Bethlehem, in fact, means house of bread, and
this is the bread that came forth in Bethlehem, that coming

---

15 Cyril of Alexandria, *Commentary upon the Gospel according to St. Luke* on Luke 2:7, trans.
R. Payne Smith (Oxford: Oxford University Press, 1859), 11–12.

16 John Chrysostom, *Homilies on First Corinthians* 24.8, in *Nicene and Post-Nicene Fathers of
the Christian Church: First Series*, 14 vols., ed. Philip Schaff (New York: Christian Literature,
1889), 12:143 (hereafter cited as *Nicene and Post-Nicene Fathers*).

17 Origen, *Fragments in Luke* 40a, in *Mysterium Ecclesiae: Images of the Church and Its Members in Origin*, by Fred Ledegang (Leuven: Leuven University Press, 2001), 309.

down from heaven, was made for us; the bread into whose mystery angels desire [to look].[18]

In addition, Gregory the Great says something similar in a homily he preached in the late 500s:

Bethlehem is translated "house of bread," and it is he who said: "I am the living bread who came down from heaven" [John 6:51]. The place in which the Lord was born was called the "house of bread" because it was truly going to come to pass that he would appear there in a material body who would nourish the hearts of his chosen ones by an interior food.[19]

These writers intend to show us that *we enter into the mystery of what happened on Christmas through the Eucharist.*

The Origins of Midnight Mass

In the Gospel of Luke, Jesus' birth is heralded by angels who appear to shepherds who were "keeping watch over their flock *by night*" (Luke 2:8). It is fitting, then, that the Church celebrates "midnight mass." But why *midnight*? For the early Christians, the practice was due to their reading of Scripture.

In the book known as the Wisdom of Solomon, we read:

For while gentle silence enveloped all things,
and night in its swift course was now half gone,
your all-powerful word leaped from heaven, from the royal
    throne,
into the midst of the land that was doomed. (Wisdom
    18:14–15)

---

18 Jerome, *Homily* 64, in Ewald, *Homilies of Saint Jerome*, 54.
19 Gregory the Great, *Homily* 8 (*Patrologia Latina* 1103), trans. Dom Hurst, *Forty Gospel Homilies* (Piscataway, NJ: Gorgias Press, 2009), 51.

In the late 300s, the Church Father and Doctor John Chrysostom was apparently the first to apply this verse to the birth of Christ.[20] The nativity marked the occasion when this passage was truly fulfilled: God's "all-powerful word leaped from heaven." Since Wisdom says this happened when night was "half gone," it was fitting to link Jesus' birth to midnight.

For many, the humble appearance of the eucharistic bread and wine is a scandal. How can Christ really be present in such ordinary food? The answer to this question is found in the manger. Christ is willing to be laid where the animals eat. So too, he is ready to come to us. The idea that he was born at midnight further emphasizes Christ's humility—rather than marking his arrival with a bang, he enters the world in the middle of the night, when most are fast sleep. The momentous event of the Messiah's coming passes in silence. He is simply laid quietly among the animals.

Christians are fond of pointing out that there can be no "Christmas" without "Christ." Just as we ought to be aware of taking "Christ" out of "Christmas," we should also guard against taking the "Mass" out of "Christmas." The central meaning of the Christmas story is that heaven has touched down to earth in Christ. This message is not simply about a *past* event. Christ continues to come to us when we receive him in the Church's liturgy. Christmas is incomplete without entering into the mystery that continues to be made present in the eucharistic worship of the Church. There the peace announced by the angels can be found.

But what does the "peace" promised at Christmas really involve? And why are angels the ones who announce it? That is the focus of our next chapter.

---

20 Joseph F. Kelly, *The Origins of Christmas*, rev. ed. (Collegeville, MN: Liturgical Press, 2014), 86.

8

"Angels We Have Heard on High": The Shepherds in the Field

Angels are frequently associated with Christmas. Whether in pageants as costumed children, on greeting cards, or on decorations, angels are everywhere. For anyone familiar with the New Testament accounts of Jesus' birth, the use of angel imagery at Christmas makes perfect sense. As we have seen, in the Gospel of Luke the angel Gabriel visits Zechariah and Mary. In addition, Matthew has an unnamed angel speak to Joseph in a dream.

Going on, Luke's account of the night of Jesus' birth involves not just one angel but "a multitude of the heavenly host" (Luke 2:13) who appear to shepherds. The scene is famously portrayed in the classic carol "Angels We Have Heard on High," whose English words were penned by James Chadwick in 1882.

> Angels we have heard on high
> Sweetly singing o'er the plains
> And the mountains in reply
> Echoing their joyous strains
> Gloria in excelsis Deo!

The last line, "Gloria in excelsis Deo," which is Latin for "Glory to God in the highest," is used in churches every Sunday.

In this chapter, we will examine the role of the angels in Jesus' birth. Why do they come to shepherds? Why are angels the ones who announce the birth of the Messiah? And how are we to understand the angelic message of "good tidings" and "peace on earth"?

Why Shepherds?

After describing how Jesus was born in Bethlehem and laid in a manger, Luke says: "Now in that same region there were shepherds out in the field, keeping watch over their flock by night" (Luke 2:8). Why are shepherds so important?

He Has Raised Up the Lowly

Contrary to what you may have heard, shepherds were not especially held in disdain by ancient Jews as uncouth or unclean. Heroes of Israel's past such as Moses had been shepherds (see Exodus 3:1). Still, shepherds were among the poor and lowly. For Luke, this makes them perfect candidates to receive "the good news."

When Mary visits Elizabeth, she breaks out in a song of praise:

> [God] has looked upon the lowliness of his handmaid....
> He has done a mighty deed with his arm;
> He has scattered the proud in the imagination of their
>   hearts.
> He has brought down the rulers from their thrones,
> And has exalted the lowly.
> He has filled the hungry with good things;
> And the rich he has sent away empty. (Luke 1:48, 51–53)

Mary gives voice to a theme that runs throughout the Gospel of Luke: God raises up the lowly and the humble while bringing down the rich and the powerful who are arrogant of heart. This is key to understanding the role of the shepherds in Jesus' birth.

The Shepherd King as the King of Shepherds

Especially relevant for Luke's story is the fact that David, the man who put Bethlehem on the map, was himself a shepherd (1 Samuel 16:11). That God called a mere shepherd boy to reign over Israel is a theme highlighted in the biblical books. Later, the Lord reminds David of his simple origins, saying, "I took you from the pasture, from following the sheep to be prince over my people Israel" (2 Samuel 7:8).

In recounting Jesus' birth, Luke highlights the way God continues to use the unlikely. He begins by recounting how Caesar had issued a decree that involved the enrollment of "all the world" (Luke 2:1). But the true King, like David, emerges from obscurity. He does not even have his own bed; he is laid in a manger. Caesar may reign, but he is clueless as to what is occurring in his kingdom. The poor shepherds, however, will know what the emperor does not—the world is about to be turned upside down.

Tidings of Comfort and Joy

At first, it is a single angel who appears to the shepherds. Like Zechariah earlier (Luke 1:12), the shepherds' first reaction to the angel is fear. Yet the heavenly messenger comforts them, making known to them "good tidings of great joy" (Luke 2:10). What is so "joyful" about his announcement?

The Proclamation of the King's Birth

In Luke, the angel tells the shepherds:

> Do not be afraid, for behold, I bring to you *good tidings* of
> great joy, which shall be for all the people. For unto you is
> born this day in the city of David a *savior* who is Christ the
> Lord. And this shall be a sign to you: you shall find the baby
> wrapped in swaddling clothes and lying in a manger. (Luke
> 2:10–12)

The angel is quick to comfort the shepherds; they are not to be
afraid. Instead, he announces, "I bring to you good tidings."
What are these "good tidings"? The Christ—the Messiah—
has been born. The true King has arrived.

The language used by the angel seems to have an important
subtext. An ancient inscription that dates to 9 B.C. heralds the
birthday of Caesar Augustus with words that are strikingly
similar to those used by the angel:

> Providence, which has ordered all things and is deeply inter-
> ested in our life, has set in most perfect order by giving us
> Augustus, whom she filled with virtue that he might benefit
> humankind, sending him as a *savior* ... that he might end war
> and arrange all things, and since he, Caesar, by his appear-
> ance (excelled even our anticipations), surpassing all previous
> benefactors, and not even leaving to posterity any hope of
> surpassing what he has done, and since the birthday of *the god
> Augustus* was the beginning of *the good tidings* [*euangeliōn*] for
> the world that came by reason of him.[1]

---

1   Translation from Craig A. Evans, "Mark's Incipit and the Priene Calendar Inscription: From
Jewish Gospel to Greco-Roman Gospel," *Journal of Greco-Roman Judaism and Christianity* 1
(2000): 67–81.

Scholars note various parallels between the way Caesar's birth is announced in this inscription and what is said about Christ's birth by the angel in Luke:

Roman Description of Caesar's Birth	The Angel's Message of Jesus' Birth
To "benefit humankind"	Issued "to all the people"
Caesar is "savior"	Christ is "savior"
"good tidings"	"I bring to you good tidings"

According to the angel, what imperial propaganda attributes to Caesar is actually realized in Christ.

The Gospel writers reveal that hopes for salvation are not to be pegged on political figures. As I frequently point out to my students, Jesus lost the only election in which he was up for a vote; the crowd chose Barabbas instead of Christ. Barabbas' name is significant; it literally means "son of the father" (from the Aramaic words *bar* ["son of"] and *abba* ["father"]). Barabbas is therefore portrayed as a kind of counterfeit "son of God." According to Mark, he had been arrested in an insurrection (Mark 15:7). In other words, Barabbas represents the notion that Israel's hopes will be realized through *political violence*. Jesus, however, shows that sinners are to be redeemed not by killing them but by suffering for them. Instead of taking matters into his own hands, Christ surrenders himself into the hands of others.

In Greek, the angel's announcement, "I bring to you good tidings" (*euangelizomai*), uses the verbal form of the Greek word translated "good news" or "gospel" (*euangelion*). The shepherds, therefore, hear the "gospel": the Christ has come, and he is the true Savior.

The Gospel of Joy

The theme of joy permeates the Gospel of Luke. When Gabriel greets Mary, he literally tells her, "*Rejoice [chaire]*, full of grace, the Lord is with you" (Luke 1:28). The traditional translation, "Hail," is not inaccurate. But it does unfortunately obscure this meaning: Mary is to be joyful because God is present to her.

Joy is especially associated with turning away from sin in repentance. Jesus says, "There is joy in the presence of the angels of God over one sinner who repents" (Luke 15:10). Later in the Gospel, the tax collector Zacchaeus receives Jesus with "joy" (Luke 19:6) before renouncing his sinful ways. The joy highlighted in the Gospel message, then, is ultimately anchored in the notion of reconciliation with God. This leads us to a related idea proclaimed by the angels: "peace."

Heaven's Army and Peace on Earth

After having heard the "good tidings of great joy" that "Christ the Lord" has been born (Luke 2:11), the heavens are filled with the sound of angelic choruses:

> And suddenly there was with the angel a multitude of the heavenly host praising God, and saying, "Glory to God in the highest, and peace on earth to men with whom he is pleased." (Luke 2:13–14)

Here we can note two things. First, the appearance of a "host" of angels. Second, that "peace on earth" is given not simply to all, but to those "with whom [God] is pleased." Here let us consider these aspects of Luke's account.

The Heavenly "Host"

Luke says that "a multitude of the heavenly host" appeared to the shepherds. The word "host" can easily be misunderstood. In English, the term can refer to someone who receives or entertains guests. That is not the word's meaning here. The Greek word translated "host" (*stratia*) means military forces; here the shepherds have a vision of the heavenly *army*.

Angelic soldiers are found throughout the Scriptures. For example, in the Old Testament we read a story in which the prophet Elisha and his servant are surrounded by enemy troops. When the young man with him begins to fear, Elisha comforts him by saying, "Fear not, for those who are with us are more than those who are with them" (2 Kings 6:16). After Elisha prays that his servant's eyes will be opened, the young man sees that "the mountain *was full of horses and chariots of fire* around Elisha" (2 Kings 6:17). In the end, Elisha is delivered.

The shepherds' vision of the Lord's heavenly troops makes the point that God is the true King. Whereas Caesar seeks to manifest his power through force, the Lord's armies remain invisible. They come to sing of peace. In this, the meekness of the newborn King is stressed. His soldiers may not be seen, but they are nonetheless real. They could easily deliver Jesus from his enemies. Jesus, however, refuses to display his glory and summon the angelic powers that are at his beck and call (cf. Luke 4:9–11). Jesus will not conquer by displays of power and might but by suffering in love.

Glory to God in the Highest

How do the angelic armies, then, engage in battle? Through worship. There is no mention here of angelic swords. The "host" of angels is fully occupied in "praising God and saying, 'Glory to God in the highest'" (Luke 2:13–14).

At the appearance of the first angel, we read, "The glory of the Lord shone around" (Luke 2:9). In the Scriptures, the appearance of God's glory is especially linked with the tabernacle and the temple, that is, the places where Israel worships the Lord.[2] At the climax of the book of Exodus, we read that "the glory of the LORD filled the tabernacle" (Exodus 40:34). Later, Isaiah will have a vision of the Lord in the temple, in which he sees the seraphim calling to one another: "Holy, holy, holy is the LORD of hosts; the whole earth is full of his glory!" (Isaiah 6:3). The revelation of God's glory to the shepherds on the night of Christ's nativity shows us what is happening in Bethlehem: heaven is coming to earth in the manger; the Lord has come.

The glorious truth of the child's identity might be hinted at by the angel's original announcement: "For unto you is born this day" (Luke 2:11). The line seems to evoke Isaiah 9:

> For unto us a child is born,
>   unto us a son is given ...
>   and his name shall be called
> "Wonderful Counselor, *Mighty God*,
>   Everlasting Father, Prince of Peace." (Isaiah 9:6–7)

The Mighty God has arrived in the coming of Jesus.

The Birthday of Peace

Finally, we note that the angels declare: "Peace on earth among those with whom he is pleased [*eudokias*]" (Luke 2:14). The

---

2   Raymond E. Brown, *The Birth of the Messiah: New Updated Edition* (New Haven, CT: Yale University Press, 1993), 426.

specificity—"with whom he is pleased"—is important. Older translations simply have the angels say, "Peace on earth and good will towards men." Yet this reading is based on less reliable manuscripts of Luke's Gospel. The angels' message is not that peace will be found among *all* peoples. Rather, they proclaim that peace is found among those *with whom God is pleased*.

Yet with whom is God "pleased"? Luke later shows us. At his baptism, the Spirit comes down upon Jesus and a voice is heard from heaven: "You are my beloved Son, *with you I am well pleased [eudokēsa]*" (Luke 3:22). Christ models what the person who pleases God must be like. To find peace, we must become like Christ.

This prompts another question: What does "peace" mean? According to Augustine, peace is "the tranquility of order."[3] Where there is order, there is peace; where things are disordered, there is not. Peace, then, is not simply the absence of conflict. The Romans could boast of putting down their enemies. Yet the *pax Romana*—the "Roman peace"—was not true peace. That can only be found where all things are rightly ordered. Caesar's brutal policies and self-exaltation were not about true order. Rather, it is in Christ that all things are set right with God and man. In fact, the angels' presence can be seen as pointing to this.

In a Christmas homily delivered in the late 500s, Gregory the Great focuses on the significance of the angels in Scripture. Adam and Eve, he points out, were exiled from God's presence in the Garden of Eden after their sin. They were prevented from returning to the garden by cherubim. Genesis tells us: "At the east of the garden of Eden [God] placed the cherubim, and a flaming sword that turned back and forth, to guard the way to the tree of life" (Genesis 3:24). Gregory, like

---

3   Augustine, *City of God* 19.13.1.

other interpreters before him, understands the cherubim to be heavenly beings—that is, angels.

Yet, going on, Gregory observes that due to Christ's birth, the relationship between angels and humans has changed:

> Before the Redeemer was born in the flesh, there was discord between us and the angels.... Because through sin we had become strangers to God, the angels as God's subjects cut us off from their fellowship.... Because the King of heaven has taken unto himself the flesh of our earth, the angels from their heavenly heights no longer look down upon our infirmity. Now they are at peace with us, putting away the remembrance of ancient discord.[4]

Christ brings heaven and earth into harmony. The presence of the heavenly host singing "peace" to the shepherds manifests this.

Christmas is a time for joy and peace first and foremost because we celebrate being reconciled to God in Christ; we have peace with the Lord. Citing Ephesians' teaching that Christ is "our peace" (Ephesians 2:14), in the mid-400s Leo the Great declares: "*The birthday of the Lord is the birthday of peace.*"[5] Despite whatever strife we find in the world, in Christ we are assured of peace. As Jesus tells the disciples in the Gospel of John, "I have said these things to you so that you may have peace in me. In the world you have tribulation; but have courage, I have overcome the world" (John 16:33).

In the Church's worship, the peace and joy of heaven is also made present in a unique way. As we saw in the last chapter, Christian tradition recognizes that the manger points us to the

---

4   Gregory the Great, *Homilies on the Gospels* 8.2, trans. and ed. M. F. Toal, in *The Sunday Sermons of the Great Fathers*, 4 vols. (Chicago: Henry Regnery, 1958).

5   Leo the Great, *Sermon* 26.5, in *Nicene and Post-Nicene Fathers: Second Series*, 12:138; emphasis added.

Eucharist, where the Lord is present to his people. The Church is "Bethlehem"—it is the "house of bread," the bread from heaven. Every eucharistic celebration is a kind of "little Christmas." For this reason, the Sunday liturgy is marked by the singing of the very hymn sung by the angels: "Glory to God in the highest!" With ears of faith, we hear once again in the liturgy the same angels who were present in the field as we join in their song. Heaven and earth are joined in joyful worship.

The joy we enter into is no mere fleeting emotion. Nor is it something we muster up by pretending there are no sorrows in life. First Peter tells us: "Rejoice *insofar* as you are sharing in the sufferings of Christ, that you may also rejoice and be glad when his glory is revealed" (1 Peter 4:13). In suffering, we are united to Christ, whom Luke identifies with the Servant of Isaiah, "*a man of sorrows*" (Isaiah 53:3; cf. 53:12; Luke 22:37).

In a particular way, as we have seen, Luke links joy to repentance. One of the most appropriate ways to enter into the mystery of Christ's birth, therefore, is to take the opportunity to confess our sins and avail ourselves of the mercy of God. In Catholic tradition, this is especially found in the Sacrament of Reconciliation, in which we believers do what the Letter of James teaches: "Confess your sins to one another" (James 5:16). Only by acknowledging our sins and repenting of them can we enter into the joy of the Christmas season. Christ saves us from the life of sin that leads us to exile. In fact, this was a lesson some early Christian writers detected in the story of the magi. We now examine the magi's role in the story of Jesus' birth.

9

"Star of Wonder": The Mysterious Magi

Christmas has become the preeminent time of year for gift-giving. Although this aspect of the Christmas season can become warped by consumerism, the idea of giving gifts is certainly related to the story of Jesus' birth in the New Testament. In Matthew, we read about a mysterious group of travelers who come bearing gifts, namely, the "magi."

Though they are never called "kings" in Matthew's Gospel, the magi are frequently depicted as royalty. Most famously, their story is told in the familiar carol "We Three Kings," which was written by John Henry Hopkins in 1857. Among other things, the song highlights the way the magi follow the famous "Christmas star" to the place of Jesus' birth. In the lyrics, they are portrayed as singing:

> O star of wonder, star of night
> Star with royal beauty bright.
> Westward leading, still proceeding
> Guide us to thy perfect light.

In subsequent verses, the song details the gifts the magi bring to Jesus: gold, frankincense, and myrrh.

The story of the magi raises lots of questions. Who are they? Why are they portrayed as kings in Christian tradition?

What is the star? And what is "frankincense"? Here we will answer these questions. As we shall see, the story of the magi points beyond itself and reminds us of the reason Christ was born in the first place—to save God's people.

Who Are the Magi?

In Matthew's Gospel, the magi make their first appearance in Jerusalem, announcing the birth of a new king:

> Now after Jesus was born in Bethlehem of Judea in the days of Herod the king, behold, magi came from the east to Jerusalem, saying, "Where is he who is born King of the Jews? For we have seen his star at its rising and have come to worship him." (Matthew 2:1–2)

What are "magi," and why does Matthew tell us the story of their visit?

Magi in the Ancient World

The word "magi" is plural, not singular. It comes to us through the Latinization of the Greek noun *magos* (singular). The Greek word had different meanings in ancient literature.[1] It could refer to religious figures who came from Media and rose to prominence in the Persian Empire. Greek and Roman writers also mention magi from Babylon. In the Greek translation of the Old Testament, the magi in Babylon are grouped

---

1   See discussion and sources in Craig S. Keener, *Acts: An Exegetical Commentary*, 4 vols. (Grand Rapids, MI: Baker Academic, 2014), 2:1502.

together with the "wise men" and enchanters (Daniel 2:10, 27). This is the reason the term "wise men" can be applied to the magi in Matthew.

The term could simply mean "those who possessed superior knowledge and ability, including astrologers, oriental sages, and soothsayers in general."[2] The magi who visit Jesus are therefore sometimes interpreted as representing the wise and virtuous pagans who were searching for God's truth.

For Jews, however, the "magi" were not necessarily benevolent. Readers will probably pick up on the connection between "magi" and "magic." In Jewish works, magi are often identified as sorcerers.[3] According to the law, individuals who practiced sorcery were to be put to death (Exodus 22:18; Deuteronomy 13:10; cf. 18:10). For many ancient Jews, the use of magic was linked to the occult and demonic powers.[4] Many non-Jews, however, were dismissive of "magic," attributing it to superstition or fraud. In some works, therefore, magi are viewed as charlatans.

In the book of the Acts of the Apostles, the various negative views of magi seem to sit alongside one another. In Acts 8, we encounter a *magos* named Simon who is said to be capable of performing amazing deeds (Acts 8:9–11). Here it would seem that a *magos* is portrayed as having the ability to do spectacular works through the power of evil. Later in Acts, Paul has a run-in with another *magos*, "a Jewish false prophet," who is known by two names, "Bar-Jesus" and "Elymas" (Acts 13:4–8). The Apostle Paul condemns him, saying: "You son of the devil, you enemy of all righteousness, *full of all deceit* and wickedness, will you not stop making crooked the straight

---

2   W. D. Davies and Dale C. Allison Jr., *The Gospel according to Saint Matthew*, 3 vols. (London: T&T Clark International, 2004), 1:228.

3   Daniel 2:2, 10, LXX; *T. Reub.* 4:9; Philo, *Special Laws* 3:93.

4   Damascus Document[a] (CD) 5:18.

paths of the Lord?" (Acts 13:10). Here the magician is portrayed as both wicked and deceitful—that is, fraudulent.

The Significance of the Magi in Matthew

While it is theoretically possible that Matthew's magi are
Jewish like Elymas in Acts, three details make this extremely
unlikely. First, they are described as coming "from the east"
(Matthew 2:1). Second, after they visit the infant Jesus, "they
departed to their own country" (Matthew 2:12). If the magi
were Jews, it would seem odd to call a Gentile territory "their
own country." Finally, the magi come seeking the "King of
the Jews." Jews preferred to use the title "King of *Israel*"
(1 Samuel 24:14; Proverbs 1:1; John 1:49).[5] Later in Matthew,
the Romans call Jesus "King of the Jews" (Matthew 27:29,
37), while Jewish bystanders at the Cross use the expression
"King of Israel" (Matthew 27:42).

By including Gentiles in the nativity story of Jesus,
Matthew points forward to what happens at the end of the
Gospel—Jesus sends the twelve out to make disciples of "all
nations" (Matthew 28:19). Early Christian writers therefore
maintain that the magi's coming points to the way the Messiah's birth signals the salvation of all humanity.

Although the magi are likely non-Jews, Matthew never
tells us their precise origin. Parthia or Persia would be a natural guess. Early Christian depictions tend to portray them
as coming from Persia. This understanding ended up saving
the famed Church of the Nativity in Bethlehem in A.D. 614.
When Persian soldiers sacked the city, they burned churches
down. However, when they came into the Church of the

---

5   Dale C. Allison Jr., *Constructing Jesus: Memory, Imagination, and History* (Grand Rapids, MI:
Baker Academic, 2010), 235.

Nativity, the soldiers saw a mosaic that portrayed the magi as Persians. For that reason, the invaders spared the church.[6]

Still, it is not certain that the magi were Persians. The earliest sources that identify them, including Justin Martyr and Tertullian, say the magi came from Arabia.[7] Alternatively, a Babylonian connection might be viewed as fitting given the Jewish exile to Babylon—something Matthew mentions in the first chapter of his Gospel. Nevertheless, since Matthew never tells us where they came from, any conclusion about their origin must be held tentatively.

The inclusion of magi at the scene of Jesus' birth may also be a sign that God will include in his kingdom those who have been associated with evil and deceit. Just as he would later dine with known sinners such as tax collectors and call them to follow him (Matthew 9:9–13), so even in his infancy Jesus draws the magi to himself.

Writing in the mid-200s, the early Christian scholar Origen offers this interpretation of the magi's significance:

> Magi are in communion with demons and by their formulas invoke them for the ends that they desire; and they succeed in these practices so long as nothing more divine and potent than the demons and the spell that invokes them appears or is pronounced. But if anything more divine were to appear, the powers of the demons would be destroyed.... *The effect of [Jesus' birth] was that the demons lost their strength and became weak; their sorcery was confuted and their power overthrown....* Accordingly, when the magi wanted to perform their usual practices, which they had previously effected by certain charms and trickery, they tried to find out the reason why they no longer worked, concluding that it was an important

---

6   See Raymond E. Brown, *The Birth of the Messiah: New Updated Edition* (New Haven, CT: Yale University Press, 1993), 168.

7   Justin Martyr, *Dialogue with Trypho* 77; Tertullian, *Against Marcion* 3.113.

one. Seeing a sign from God in heaven, they wished to see
what was indicated by it.[8]

The interpretation offered by Origen obviously goes beyond
what Matthew explicitly says. Nonetheless, it makes the
essential point that in the magi's search for Jesus we might be
able to detect a reference to Christ's superiority and defeat of
demonic powers.

The Magi as Kings and the Imagery of Camels

In manger scenes and in art, the magi are often portrayed as
three kings riding on camels. Later sources would even assign
names to the magi (see below). Yet Matthew never tells us
how many of them there were, that they were royalty, how
they traveled, or what their names were. From where, then,
do these things come to us?

First, many suppose that the reason the magi came to be
viewed as a group of three is because Matthew describes them
as bringing three gifts to Jesus: gold, frankincense, and myrrh
(Matthew 2:11). The earliest writer to portray the magi as a
triad, however, was the early Christian scholar Origen, who
never mentions the three gifts. Origen believes Jesus' Gentile
visitors are foreshadowed in a story found in the book of Genesis: three pagans visit Isaac, the son of Abraham, seeking to
establish a covenant with him (Genesis 26:26).[9] Origen notes
aspects of the Genesis narrative that have parallels with Matthew's account of the magi:

---

8   Origen, *Contra Celsum* 1.60, trans. Henry Chadwick (Cambridge: Cambridge University
Press, 1953), 54–55.
9   Origen, *Homilies on Genesis* 14.3.

The Pagans Who Visit Isaac (Genesis 26)	The Magi Who Visit Christ (Matthew 1–2)
"We see plainly"	"They saw the star.... They saw the child"
"The Lord is with you"	Christ is "God with us"
Genesis 26:28	*Matthew 2:10–11; 1:23*

From Origen on, Christian tradition would portray the magi as a group of three. Later writers would identify them as a group of three because of their three gifts.

Second, the idea that the magi are "kings" who come riding on "camels" emerges from Old Testament passages that scholars view as "implicit" in Matthew's narrative.[10] The magi's gifts of "gold" and "frankincense" are reminiscent of Isaiah's vision of Israel's future restoration:

A multitude of *camels* shall cover you,
the young male *camels* of Midian and Ephah;
all those from Sheba shall come.
They shall bring *gold* and *frankincense*,
and shall proclaim the praise of the LORD...
Sons of a foreign country shall build up your walls,
and their *kings* shall minister to you ...
that men may bring to you the wealth of the nations,
with their *kings* led in procession. (Isaiah 60:6, 10–11)

This passage was seen by early Christian writers as foreshadowing the magi's visit. Since those who bring gifts of "gold"

---

10 Brown, *Birth of the Messiah*, 179.

and "frankincense" in Isaiah are "kings" who come with "camels," Isaiah's oracles were merged with Matthew's story. Nativity scenes, therefore, that portray the magi as kings riding on camels are essentially proclaiming that their visit was prophesied in Isaiah.

The tradition of portraying the magi as "kings" is related to another Old Testament passage: Psalm 72. Here the psalmist speaks of how foreign kings will come and bring gifts to the son of David. The version of this psalm in the Greek translation of the Old Testament contains some important parallels with Matthew's narrative:

> *Kings* of Tharsis and of the isles will *offer gifts*,
> *Kings* of Arabs and Saba will supply *gifts*!
> And all the *kings* will *worship* him,
> all nations serve him! (Psalm 72:10–11)

This psalm was easily interpreted as a prophecy about Jesus, who is clearly presented as the son of David in Matthew. The scene of the magi's visit in Matthew evokes aspects of the psalm:

The Kings in Psalm 72	The Magi in Matthew 2
Kings "offer" (*prosoisousin*)	Magi "offer" (*prospherō*)
"gifts" (*dōra*) to son of David	"gifts" (*dōra*) to Christ
... "worship" (*proskynēsousin*) the son of David	... "worship" (*prosekynēsan*) Christ
Psalm 72 (71):10, 11	*Matthew 2:11*

Furthermore, the psalm says the king will "save" (*sōsei*) the poor and "redeem" (*lytrōsetai*) his people (Psalm 71:13–14,

LXX), using words Matthew uses for Jesus—he will *"save [sōsei] his people"* (Matthew 1:21) by giving his life as a "ransom *[lytron]* for many" (Matthew 20:28). The magi can therefore be viewed as fulfilling the vision of Psalm 72.

The Magi in Tradition

The earliest attempt to name the magi is found in an anonymous source from Alexandria, Egypt, which can be dated to the 500s. There the three travelers are called "Bithisarea, Melchior, and Gaspar." Later in the same century a slightly modified version of these names is included in a mosaic found in a church located in Ravenna, Italy. Here they are said to be "Balthassar, Melchior, and Gaspar." These names underwent further development. An "s" was dropped from "Balthassar," and "Gaspar" became "Caspar." "Balthasar" might come from "Belteshazzar," the prophet Daniel's Babylonian name (Daniel 1:7). "Melchior" may come for the Hebrew words for "king" and "light." "Caspar" could be an allusion to an Indian king. Yet no one knows for sure how these names were chosen.[11]

Other traditions also emerge. Syriac sources such as the *Revelation of the Magi* say there were *twelve* different magi, providing names for all of them. Nevertheless, the Syriac sources do not all agree on the details of their identities.[12]

Finally, a passage that for a long time was wrongly attributed to the English writer Bede offers this description of the magi:

---

11 For more, see Joseph F. Kelly, *The Feast of Christmas* (Collegeville, MN: Liturgical Press, 2010), 31.

12 For a discussion, see Witold Witakowski, "The Magi in Syriac Tradition," in *Malphono w-Rabo d-Malphone: Studies in Honor of Sebastian P. Brock* (Piscataway, NJ: Gorgias Press, 2008), 809–43.

The first is said to have been Melchior, an old man with white hair and a long beard ... who offered gold to the Lord as to a king. The second, Gaspar by name, young and beardless and ruddy complexioned ... honored him as God by his gift of incense, an oblation worthy of divinity. The third, black-skinned and heavily bearded, named Balthasar ... by his gift of myrrh testified to the Son of Man who was to die.[13]

This account seems to have shaped subsequent Christian imagination. Depictions of the magi usually present them in ways inspired by this explanation, highlighting the way they represent the peoples from all over the world.

Yet perhaps even more fascinating to readers than the magi has been another part of their story: the Christmas star. We now turn to consider this aspect of Matthew's presentation.

The Christmas Star

The "star of Bethlehem" features prominently in Christmas iconography. But why a star? And what was it?

The Insufficiency of the Star

In ancient literature, astronomical signs were associated with major events. According to Virgil, Aeneas was led by a star to the place where Rome was to be founded.[14] The ancient Roman historian Suetonius reports that the birth of Augustus was heralded by a portent that was interpreted as announcing

---

13 Cited by Brown, *Birth of the Messiah*, 199.
14 Virgil, *Aeneid* 2.694.

the birth of a new king.[15] The Jewish historian Josephus links the destruction of Jerusalem to the appearance of a star that had the shape of a sword. He also writes about a comet that continued for an entire year.[16] For Matthew's readers, it would not have been at all surprising to hear that the birth of the Messiah coincided with a celestial sign.

Here we might note a contrast between what we find in Matthew and Luke. Whereas in Luke the Jewish shepherds of Bethlehem are informed of the Messiah's birth by angels, the magi hear no voice. Instead, they follow what seems to be a natural sign, a star. Ancient Christian writers saw this as fitting. Gregory the Great, for example, observed that Gentiles do not have divine revelation in the Scriptures; it was therefore appropriate that they came to know the birth of Christ through a star—that is, through a physical sign.[17]

Still, the star described by Matthew is likely not to be interpreted as some sort of ordinary natural phenomenon. Some have tried to reconstruct the precise astronomical circumstances of Jesus' birth, identifying the star as a supernova, comet, or some sort of planetary conjunction. These approaches are unconvincing because they overlook key features of the Gospel of Matthew. We are told that the star "went before [the magi] until it came and *stood over where the child was*" (Matthew 2:9). This movement is not physically possible for a star. The heavenly sign leading the magi on identifies the very place where the child Jesus is by stopping directly over it.

Chrysostom long ago pointed out that the star's description in Matthew indicates that it is not a natural star:

---

15 Suetonius, *Augustus* 94.
16 Josephus, *Jewish War* 6.289.
17 Gregory the Great, *Forty Gospel Homilies*, trans. Dom Hurst (1990; repr., Piscataway, NJ: Gorgias Press, 2009), 55.

> For you know that a spot of such small dimensions ... could
> not possibly be marked out by a star. For by reasons of its
> immense height, it could not sufficiently distinguish so con-
> fined a spot and reveal it to those who were desiring to see it. . .
> How then, tell me, did the star point out a spot so confined,
> just the space of a manger and shed, *unless it left that height
> and came down,* and *stood over the very head of the child*?[18]

One cannot give directions to a house by identifying which
star is over it. For Chrysostom the star therefore must have
descended. He even maintains it settled over Christ's head.

Church Fathers, therefore, either viewed the star's movement as directed by angels or thought the star was an angel in
disguise. This is not surprising. In ancient Jewish and Christian sources, "angels and stars go together."[19] It is no wonder,
then, that depictions of the nativity often replace the star with
an angel. The notion that it must have been a purely naturally
occurring astronomical phenomenon took root only in the
modern period as interest in the sciences grew.

One thing, however, is clear: in Matthew's account, the
star is not able to lead the magi to Jesus on its own. The magi
follow the star to Jerusalem. There they ask where the new
king is. As we have seen, it is only because Herod has the
scribes consult the Scriptures that the location of the Messiah's birthplace is known. The narrative, therefore, suggests
the limits of natural reason and the need for divine revelation.
Human intellect can help guide humanity to the truth but is
not sufficient; divine revelation is necessary. In fact, the star's
presence in Matthew's narrative makes more sense when its
connection to biblical prophecy is further understood.

---

18 Chrysostom, *Homily on Matthew* 6.2 (3), in *Studies in Matthew: Interpretation Past and Present,* by Dale C. Allison Jr. (Grand Rapids, MI: Baker Academic, 2005), 18.

19 Ibid., 25. The rest of the paragraph draws from Allison's chapter (see 17–41).

The Star and Balaam's Prophecy

The Christmas star is best interpreted as referring to a biblical prophecy. Near the end of the book of Numbers, a Gentile prophet named Balaam delivers the following oracle:

> I see him, but not now; I behold him, but not near: *a star shall come forth out of Jacob, and a scepter shall rise out of Israel*; it shall crush the forehead of Moab.... *Edom shall be dispossessed....* By Jacob shall *dominion* be exercised. (Numbers 24:17–19)

The reference to a "scepter" and to "dominion" points to the coming of a future ruler. The likelihood that Balaam is describing a coming king is further cemented by the star symbolism. In other biblical texts, rulers are associated with stars (Isaiah 14:12; Ezekiel 32:7).

That Balaam's oracle was interpreted as a messianic prophecy by ancient Jews is confirmed by the Dead Sea Scrolls. There we are told how to interpret the passage: "The scepter is *the prince of the whole congregation*."[20] As John Collins, an expert on the Dead Sea Scrolls, writes, "There can be little doubt that the prince who is identified with the scepter ... is also a messianic figure."[21]

Even though it is never explicitly quoted, ancient and modern interpreters generally agree that the star in Matthew is meant to remind the reader of Balaam's prophecy.[22] In addition, there is a feature of the prophecy that should not be

---

20 Damascus Document[a] (CD) 7:20. Slightly adapted from Florentino García Martínez and Eibert J. C. Tigchelaar, *The Dead Sea Scrolls Study Edition*, 2 vols. (Leiden: Brill, 1997), 1:569.

21 John Collins, *The Scepter and the Star: The Messiahs of the Dead Sea Scrolls and Other Ancient Literature* (New York: Doubleday, 1995), 64. See the discussion on 63–67.

22 Origen, *Against Celsus* 1.60; Jerome, *Commentary on Matthew* 2:2; Brown, *Birth of the Messiah*, 182.

passed over: "Edom shall be dispossessed" (Numbers 24:18). This seems relevant to Matthew's broader narrative. King Herod himself was an Idumean and therefore came from the land identified with Edom. The allusion to the Numbers passage seems to imply that Herod is set for a downfall—"Edom shall be dispossessed."

Balaam and the Magi

The ancient Jewish author Philo explicitly calls Balaam a *magos*, the same noun that is used for the "magi."[23] Early Christian writers apparently knew about Balaam's supposed relationship to magi and believed it was significant for understanding the birth of Jesus. According to some, the magi who visited Jesus knew of Balaam's oracle. For example, in the 310s, Eusebius writes:

> We are told *that Balaam's successors* moved by [his prediction in Numbers 24] (for the prediction was preserved most likely among them), when they noticed in the heavens a strange star besides the usual ones ... hastened to arrive at Palestine, to inquire about the King announced by the star's appearance.[24]

In their well-respected commentary on Matthew, W. D. Davies and Dale Allison conclude that Eusebius was likely on the right track: "Matthew probably thought of the magi as 'Balaam's successors' ... who come to witness the fulfillment of the [Old Testament] oracle their predecessor uttered so long ago."[25]

---

23 See Philo, *Life of Moses* 1.276; cf. 1.92.
24 Eusebius, *Demonstration of the Gospel* 9.1, trans. W. J. Ferrar (New York: Macmillan, 1920).
25 Davies and Allison, *Matthew*, 1:231.

The Cradle and the Cross

No treatment of the magi would be complete without a discussion of their three gifts. What exactly was "frankincense"? And what are we to make of the story that concludes the magi's visit, namely, the horrific story of Herod's slaughter of the innocent children in Bethlehem? Why would Matthew include this detail in the otherwise joyful story of Christ's birth?

The Gifts of the Magi

When the magi finally arrive at Jesus' birthplace, they are said to "worship" him.

> And when they came into the house, they saw the child with Mary his mother, and fell down, and worshipped him, and opening their treasure chests, they offered him gifts of gold, and frankincense, and myrrh. (Matthew 2:11)

The Greek verb Matthew uses to describe the magi's act of "worshipping" (*proskyneō*) Jesus is worth talking about. The word can simply refer to the homage given to a king (1 Chronicles 29:20). Within the larger narrative of Matthew, however, the scene seems to point to more than just his identity as the king from David's line. As we have seen, in the Gospel, Jesus is truly "God with us" (Matthew 1:23). It is no wonder, then, that he is "worshipped."

The three gifts given to Jesus are each of immense value.[26] Frankincense is essentially "incense." It was made from the

---

26 For what follows, see ibid., 1:249–51; Ulrich Luz, *Matthew*, Hermeneia, 3 vols. (Minneapolis: Fortress Press, 2007), 1:114–15.

resin of trees and was imported from Arabia (Jeremiah 6:20) for use in religious worship (Exodus 30:4–8; Leviticus 24:7). Myrrh was the resin of myrrh trees, which were found especially in Arabia and Ethiopia. Like frankincense, myrrh was used in religious worship. It was also associated with magic and wedding ceremonies. In addition, it had other uses, including cosmetic and medicinal purposes. These gifts, as we have seen, are associated with the age of Israel's restoration in Isaiah 60:1–14. Jesus' coming fulfills such hopes. The gifts might be seen as proof of the magi's Arabian background, but since such goods were traded, the magi are not necessarily Arabian.

Plotting against the King of the Jews

Later Christian writers would find deeper significance in the magi's gifts. According to many—including Irenaeus, Clement of Alexandria, and Origen—the gold points to Jesus' royal identity, the frankincense signifies his divinity, and the myrrh anticipates his death.[27] The latter interpretation is rooted in the report of Jesus' burial found not in Matthew but in John. There we read that, after his Crucifixion, those who buried Jesus did so using "a mixture of myrrh" (John 19:39). Unlike John and Mark (cf. Mark 15:23), Matthew does not mention myrrh in connection with Jesus' Passion or death. Nevertheless, Matthew's account of Jesus' birth does contain elements that foreshadow Jesus' Passion.

When the magi appear in Jerusalem, they ask, "Where is he who is born *King of the Jews*?" (Matthew 2:2). This title reappears in Matthew's account of Jesus' Passion. Pilate asks

---

27 Irenaeus, *Against Heresies* 3.9.2; Clement of Alexandria, *Christ the Educator* 2.8.63; 5; Origen, *Against Celsus* 1.60.

Jesus: "Are you the *King of the Jews*?" (Matthew 27:11). Later, Jesus is mocked by the Roman soldiers who place a crown of thorns on his head and kneel before him, mocking him by declaring: "Hail, *King of the Jews*!" (Matthew 27:29). Finally, when Jesus is crucified, the Romans place a sign over his head that reads: "This is Jesus the *King of the Jews*" (Matthew 27:37).

In addition, Herod's response to the arrival of the magi seems to anticipate what happens in Jesus' Passion. When the magi come, Herod assembles the religious leaders: "And *gathering together* all the chief priests and scribes of the people, he inquired from them where the Christ was to be born" (Matthew 2:4). Strikingly, the same Greek verb translated "gathering together" (*synagō*) is used repeatedly in Matthew's account of Jesus' Passion.[28] The "chief priests and elders" are "gathered together" to plan Jesus' arrest (Matthew 26:3). The "scribes and elders" are then "gathered together" again at Caiaphas' house for Jesus' so-called "trial" (Matthew 26:57). Finally, after Jesus' death, the "chief priests and elders" are "gathered together" before Pilate (Matthew 27:62). In all of this, there may be an implicit allusion to the Greek version of Psalm 2, where the wicked kings and rulers are "gathered together" (*synēchthēsan*) against the Lord's "anointed one" (Psalm 2:2).

The Slaughter of the Innocents

The darkness of the Passion is further prefigured in the scene that follows the magi's visit. When the magi are warned in a dream about Herod's evil designs, they depart without reporting to him the Messiah's whereabouts. We read:

---

28 Brown, *Birth of the Messiah*, 174–75.

> Then Herod, when he saw that he had been deceived by the
> magi, was very angry, and he sent, and murdered all the chil-
> dren in Bethlehem, and in all the region around it, from two
> years old and under, according to the time which he had dil-
> igently inquired from the magi. (Matthew 2:16)

A few things should be said here.

First, contrary to what we see in most nativity scenes, the
shepherds of Luke and the magi of Matthew show up at Jesus'
birthplace *at different times*. Herod seeks to kill the children
from two years of age and younger, which might suggest he
knows the child Jesus is not a newborn. While Luke's shepherds are said to arrive at the manger on the night of Jesus'
birth, Matthew's magi come after seeing the star heralding
Jesus' birth and traveling from some distance. It is perhaps
significant that Jesus is called an "infant" (*brephos*, Luke 2:12)
when the shepherds visit him in Luke's story, but that in the
account of the magi in Matthew a different word is used for
him; he is instead repeatedly called a "child" (*paidion*, Matthew 2:8–9, 11). The latter term in Greek can refer to a child
from eight days old to seven years of age.[29]

Second, the account of the magi is reminiscent of the story
of Moses. In various ways, Matthew's Gospel presents Jesus as
a kind of "new Moses."[30] As Pharaoh slaughtered the Hebrew
male children in the land of Egypt at the time of Moses' birth
(Exodus 1:15–21), Herod puts to death the children in Bethlehem (Matthew 2:16). As the child Moses found safety in
Egypt (Exodus 2:1–10), the Holy Family finds refuge there
(Matthew 2:13–15). As Moses eventually comes out of Egypt
(Exodus 2:15), so does Jesus (Matthew 2:19–21). And the
parallels continue from there.

---

29 D. H. Williams, "The Magi and the Star," in *The Oxford Handbook of Christmas*, ed. Timothy
Larsen (Oxford: Oxford University Press, 2020), 214.
30 See Dale C. Allison Jr., *The New Moses: A Matthean Typology* (Minneapolis: Fortress Press,
1993).

In all of this, Jesus "fulfills" the Scriptures. In a work written around the year A.D. 180, the early Christian theologian Irenaeus uses an important term for this: *recapitulation.* The short form of this word is more familiar: "recap." In Christ, the story of Israel is "summed up." Jesus is not only the new Moses, but he is also the new son of David, the new Hezekiah, and so on.

Bethlehem and the Mystery of Suffering

Finally, Herod's massacre of the children in Bethlehem makes another point: complete peace on earth does not immediately dawn with Jesus' birth. Jesus will later say the following in the Gospel of Matthew:

> Do not think that I have come to bring peace on earth; I have come not to bring peace, but a sword. For I have come to set a man against his father, and a daughter against her mother, and a daughter-in-law against her mother-in-law. (Matthew 10:34–35)

Here Jesus draws on an oracle found in the book of Micah. The prophet announces that the day of the Lord's salvation will be preceded by a period of great suffering:

> The son treats the father with contempt,
> the daughter rises up against her mother,
> the daughter-in-law against her mother-in-law;
> a man's enemies are the men of his own house. (Micah 7:6)

Jesus will bring peace and salvation, but all who follow him will also be called upon to suffer for love of him. The allegiance we are to give to Jesus must surpass that given to all others, even our fathers and mothers. Peace on earth will not be fully realized until the Second Coming. Christmas, then, must not simply be a time of worldly joy; it involves the joy and peace of Christ, which is not available apart from suffering. Luke contains a poignant reminder of this as well.

After Jesus' birth, the Holy Family goes to Jerusalem to fulfill the law's requirements (Luke 2:22–24). While there, a righteous man named Simeon rejoices when he sees the child Jesus, declaring that he will be the one to save Israel (Luke 2:26–35). Simeon, however, also warns Mary that suffering awaits her, saying, "A sword will pierce your own soul also" (Luke 2:35). Believers will also have a share in the suffering of Jesus.

During Christmas we recall how God gave us the greatest gift of all: salvation in Christ Jesus. Loving him above all things will not always make our lives easier. For one thing, it means turning away from our sinful ways, an idea that interpreters such as Origen found in the magi's gifts, which was seen as instruments of their dark magic. In the mid-400s, Leo the Great would point out that Matthew says the magi returned home by "another way" (Matthew 2:12). While this was due to the magi's desire to avoid Herod, who was enraged that they had not returned to report the whereabouts of the child (Matthew 2:16), Leo found an additional spiritual meaning in this detail: "It was proper that now believing in Christ they not walk through the paths of their old way of life, but enter upon a new path and abstain from the wanderings they left behind."[31] Christmas is a call to new life, which entails a call to repentance.

But following Christ means more than just turning from sin. It also means learning to embrace rejection and the cross of suffering. As Jesus warns: "If anyone would come after me, let him deny himself and take up his cross and follow

---

31 Leo the Great, *Sermon* 34.3, in Williams, "Magi and the Star," 216.

me" (Matthew 16:24). Yet without this cross, there can be no resurrection of the body. The slaughter of the innocent children in Bethlehem serves as a reminder of this. The Savior's coming signals redemption—but only on the other side of suffering. Like Mary, whose heart will be pierced, we too must be willing to enter into Jesus' Passion.

10

"Christ Our God to Earth Descendeth": The Historical Figure of Jesus

My all-time favorite Christmas song is "Let All Mortal Flesh Keep Silence." The hymn has its origins in the Middle Ages when it was sung in Latin as a liturgical chant. The English lyrics, written by Gerard Moultrie in 1864, begin this way:

> Let all mortal flesh keep silence,
> and with fear and trembling stand.
> Ponder nothing earthly minded,
> for with blessing in his hand,
> Christ our God to earth descendeth,
> our full homage to demand.

The words are based on a verse found in the book of Habakkuk: "But the LORD is in his holy temple; let all the earth keep silence before him" (Habakkuk 2:20). The song's message is clear: "Christ our God to earth descendeth"—God has become flesh. The world's response to this is stunned silence and worship.

According to some skeptics, however, the story of Jesus' nativity is anything but awe-inspiring. As they see it, it is simply a warmed-over version of pagan mythology. They insist that Jesus never really existed at all. Are the Gospels' reports purely mythological?

The Claims of Jesus Mythicists

The view that Jesus was not a real person and that the Gospels' accounts of him are simply adaptations of pagan mythical stories is sometimes called "Jesus mythicism." It has roots in antiquity. The anti-Christian writer Celsus sought to dismiss Christianity by pointing to parallels between it and other religions.[1] While it would take an entire book to rebut all the claims made by mythicists effectively, it is worth responding to a few of them.

The Gospel Story as Mythology?

One recent advocate of the mythicist approach to the Gospels is D. M. Murdoch. Her most well-known book, *The Christ Conspiracy*, was originally written under the pseudonym "Acharya S."[2] ("Acharya" means "guru" or "teacher"). Essentially, Murdoch argues that stories about Jesus' life and death in the Gospels were simply borrowed from myths about pagan gods. For example, Murdoch says that the Greek god Dionysus was born of a virgin on December 25 and was laid in a manger. We are also told that he was considered "the Only Begotten Son" and the "Anointed One." She further asserts that the term "Gospel" originally meant "God's Spell," an allusion to "magic, hypnosis, and delusion."[3] In the end, according to her, Christianity emerged out of pagan sun worship.

Murdoch's claims are outlandish, and her research has been roundly dismissed by credentialed scholars. Even Bart Ehrman, widely known as a skeptic himself, dismisses the work

---

1   Origen, *Against Celsus* 2.55–56.

2   Acharya S., *The Christ Conspiracy: The Greatest Story Ever Told* (Kempton, IL: Adventures Unlimited, 1999).

3   Ibid., 45.

of mythicists like Murdoch as fatally flawed. Of her work, he writes: "If she is serious, it is hard to believe that she has ever encountered anything resembling historical scholarship."[4]

Problems with Mythicist Approaches

Here we can speak broadly of three major problems in the work of mythicists such as Murdoch. First, many of the claims made by mythicists are flat-out false. Contrary to what Murdoch says, there are no ancient accounts of Dionysus' birth that indicate he was laid in a manger as a child. Her claim that the word "Gospel" originally had a connection to magic is preposterous. As we explained above, it comes from the Greek word that means "good news" (*euangelion*). This is par for the course in works of mythicists. Their claims cannot be backed up by reliable ancient sources.

Second, while some ancient mythologies do have parallels with the New Testament accounts, mythicists ignore the fact that certain pagan stories about ancient gods *post-date* the New Testament. In other words, there is strong evidence that as Christianity grew in popularity, stories about the gods were retold to make them look more like Jesus. So, rather than thinking that the Gospel writers copied everything they reported from pagan mythologies, there are reasons to think the opposite was often the case. Yet mythicists like Murdoch show little awareness of this.

Third, while there are similarities between the Gospel accounts and stories about other gods, stark differences remain that mythicists conveniently never mention. For example, while characters like Dionysus were identified as the offspring

4   Bart D. Ehrman, *Did Jesus Exist? The Historical Argument for Jesus of Nazareth* (New York: HarperOne, 2012), 21.

of the gods, the accounts of how they were conceived are strik-ingly *unlike* what is found in the New Testament accounts of Jesus' birth. The parallels fail *precisely* at the most crucial point: unlike the stories about the gods, Mary's conception of Jesus is virginal, involving no physical act causing pregnancy.

Jesus in Historical Memory

The claim that the New Testament descriptions of Jesus have no basis in history is simply unfounded. There is weighty evi-dence that Jesus truly was a real historical person.[5] Moreover, it is evident that the Gospels include historical materials.

Jesus in Ancient Sources

First, references to Jesus appear outside of the Bible. The first-century Jewish historian Josephus mentions Jesus, giving no indication that he doubts his historical existence. Scholars sus-pect that some aspects of his report were likely added by later Christian copyists. Nevertheless, it is likely that Josephus did talk about Jesus. Scholars agree he said something like the following:

> At this time there appeared Jesus, a wise man. For he was a doer of startling deeds, a teacher of people who receive the truth with pleasure. And he gained a following both among many Jews and among many of Greek origin. And when Pilate, because of an accusation made by the leading men among us,

5   See my historical method and conclusions in Michael Patrick Barber, "Did Jesus Anticipate Suffering a Violent Death? The Implications of Memory Research and Dale C. Allison's Method-ology," *Journal for the Study of the Historical Jesus* 18, no. 3 (2020): 191–219.

condemned him to the cross, those who had loved him previously did not cease to do so. And up until this very day the tribe of Christians (named after him) has not died out.[6]

That Josephus knew about Jesus is confirmed by the fact that elsewhere he speaks of James, "the brother of Jesus who is called the Christ."[7]

Jesus is also mentioned by the Roman historian Tacitus (A.D. 117), who says of Christians: "Their name comes from Christ, who, during the reign of Tiberius, had been executed by the procurator Pontius Pilate."[8] Some also believe that the Roman writer Suetonius refers to Christ in a garbled way when he speaks of controversy in Rome over a man named "Chrestus,"[9] though this is uncertain. Whatever we make of Suetonius' line, the point remains: ancient writers thought Jesus really existed.

The New Testament

The claim that the New Testament Gospels contain nothing but pure mythology must also ignore features of them that suggest otherwise. For instance, the prologue to Luke's Gospel especially emphasizes the historical nature of its contents:

Inasmuch as many have attempted to compile a narrative concerning the things which have been accomplished among us, just as they were traditioned to us by those who from the beginning were eyewitnesses and ministers of the word, it

---

6   Josephus, *Antiquities of the Jews* 18.63–64, in *A Marginal Jew: Rethinking the Historical Jesus*, vol. 1, *The Roots of the Problem and the Person*, by John P. Meier (New York: Doubleday, 1991), 61.

7   *Antiquities of the Jews* 20.20.

8   Meier, *Marginal Jew*, 1:89–90.

9   Suetonius, *Lives of the Caesars, Claudius* 5.25.4 (A.D. 121).

seemed good to me also, having followed all things carefully from the beginning, to write an orderly account for you, most excellent Theophilus, so that you may know the truth concerning the things of which you have been informed. (Luke 1:1–4)

Luke's story is presented to us as a narrative of things that have been reported by *eyewitnesses*, not as a mythological account.

The Gospel of John also says it is based on eyewitness testimony. After describing Jesus' death, the evangelist writes:

The one who saw it has borne witness—his testimony is true, and he knows that he tells the truth—that you also may believe. (John 19:35)

In addition, the Gospel closes with words that indicate that it was written by someone who had witnessed Jesus' ministry:

This is the disciple who is bearing witness to these things, and who has written down these things; and we know that his testimony is true. (John 21:24)

The earliest believers understood that their beliefs about Jesus came to them through those who had seen and heard Jesus personally.

Jesus' Disciples as Witnesses

We also know that the early followers of Jesus had contact with Jesus' original disciples. In the letters of Paul, which scholars generally view as the earliest writings in the New Testament, we learn that Paul knew apostles such as Peter, who were well respected in the early Church. Paul says that Peter, James, and John "were reputed to be pillars" (Galatians 2:9).

Virtually all scholars agree that Jesus was a teacher who had disciples. The Greek word "disciple" essentially means "student." Ancient students would have been expected to remember their teacher's words. For example, one ancient teacher is said to have rebuked a student who lost his notes, reminding him, "You should have inscribed them . . . on your mind instead of on paper."[10] While that quotation comes from a Greco-Roman context, there are good reasons to think that the students of Jewish rabbis would have also been expected to remember their teacher's basic message.[11] If, as virtually all scholars agree, Jesus was a rabbi, then he would have had students who were invested in remembering what he had to say.

Moreover, our sources report that Jesus enlisted his disciples in spreading his message even while he was alive (see, e.g., Mark 6:7–13; Matthew 10:1–7; Luke 9:1–2). That Jesus sent out followers to preach is also attested by Paul (cf. 1 Corinthians 9:14). New Testament scholar Dale Allison, therefore, concludes: "It is plausible that some people were already teaching, which means in effect rehearsing, parts of the Jesus tradition before their leader was gone."[12] All of this means that there were witnesses to Jesus' teaching quite early who would have been prepared to share Jesus' message.

Jesus, then, was not a myth. What happened to Jesus in history mattered to the early Christians. Paul seems to assume that his hearers have already heard about Jesus' life. In 1 Corinthians, it seems evident that he expects the believers to know what had happened to Jesus:

---

10 Diogenes Laertius, *Lives of Eminent Philosophers* 6.1.5, trans. R. D. Hicks, Loeb Classical Library 185 (Cambridge, MA: Harvard University Press, 1925).

11 Craig S. Keener, *Christobiography: Memories, History, and the Reliability of the Gospels* (Grand Rapids, MI: Eerdmans, 2019), 428–48.

12 Dale C. Allison Jr., *Constructing Jesus: Memory, Imagination, and History* (Grand Rapids, MI: Baker Academic, 2010), 26.

> For I received from the Lord what I also handed on to you, that the Lord Jesus on the night in which he was handed over, took bread, and when he had given thanks, he broke it, and said, "This is my body which is for you. Do this in remembrance of me." (1 Corinthians 11:23–24)

Scholars routinely point out that when Paul speaks of "handing on" what happened to Jesus, he uses technical terminology for passing on traditions (cf. 1 Corinthians 11:23 with 1 Corinthians 11:2; 15:3).[13] In short, the Jesus story was anything but fiction to Paul; it was anchored in history.

The Gospels and History

The notion that the Gospels' accounts are purely mythological is unconvincing for another reason: they are not written in a style that was generally used to tell mythological stories. We cannot consider every aspect of the Gospel narratives in a detailed way. Nevertheless, it is important to consider the broader question of the genre of the Gospels and the way the Scriptures of Israel have influenced them.

The Genre of the Gospels

Anyone who steps foot inside a bookstore is immediately struck by the many kinds of books that are available. The aisles are devoted to subjects such as history, science fiction, and self-improvement. In antiquity, there was also an awareness that authors could write different types—or *genres*—of works. In general, ancient writers distinguished between three major

---

13   Joseph A. Fitzmyer, *First Corinthians*, Anchor Yale Bible 32 (New Haven, CT: Yale University Press, 2008), 436.

categories: history (Greek: *historia*), fiction (Greek: *plasma*), and myth (Greek: *mythos*). History, as one ancient writer put it, referred to "true things that actually happened."[14] In this, history was unlike the other two literary categories: fiction concerned events that *did not* happen, and myth dealt with things that *could not* happen. Myth recounted things that "are false," such as Odysseus being turned into a horse.[15]

This raises an important question: When ancient readers picked up the Gospels, to which category of literature would they assign them? Recent scholarship has demonstrated that readers would have seen them as ancient Greco-Roman biographies, a genre ancient writers referred to with the Greek term *bioi*.[16]

Genres, of course, should always be considered somewhat fluid. Authors put their own spin on the mediums they choose to use. Some ancient biographers were more interested in accuracy than others. Some would include more fanciful elements than others. In fact, historical veracity was not always the first purpose of biographers. Biographies were written to extol their subjects. If certain facts did not fit their agendas, ancient writers might exclude or even change them.[17] Despite all of this, ancient Greco-Roman biographies were usually understood to be focused on historical persons. As New Testament scholar David Aune puts it, the genre of *bioi* was "firmly rooted in historical fact rather than literary fiction."[18]

That the Gospel writers chose to write works that look like Greco-Roman biographies severely undercuts the theory that

---

14 Asclepiades in Sextus Empiricus, *Against the Grammarians* 1.263.

15 Ibid.; Quintilian, *Orator's Education* 2.4.2.

16 Richard Burridge, *What Are the Gospels? A Comparison with Graeco-Roman Biography*, 2nd ed. (Grand Rapids, MI: Eerdmans, 2004).

17 See especially Helen K. Bond, *The First Biography of Jesus: Genre and Meaning in Mark's Gospel* (Grand Rapids, MI: Eerdmans, 2020), 66–71.

18 David E. Aune, "Greco-Roman Biography," in *Greco-Roman Literature and the New Testament: Selected Forms and Genres*, ed. David E. Aune (Atlanta: Scholars Press, 1988), 125.

they should simply be read as purely mythological accounts. Aune writes:

> While the evangelists clearly had an important theological agenda, the very fact that they chose to adapt Greco-Roman biographical conventions to tell the story of Jesus indicates that they were centrally concerned to communicate what they thought really happened.[19]

As we have seen, features such as Luke's prologue indicate that the Gospel writers did not think they were writing about a nonhistorical figure.

Certain caveats need to be made here. For one thing, ancient biographers did not have the same standards as modern historians. Ancient authors did not usually have transcripts of their subjects' speeches. Writers were therefore not expected to give verbatim accounts of what was said by them. Preserving the "substance" of what was spoken was believed to be sufficient. In addition, ancient biographies often recounted events out of historical sequence. A certain "narrative elasticity" was permitted. Furthermore, biographies were not expected to be comprehensive. For instance, ancient biographers did not always feel the need to tell their readers about the birth and childhood of their subjects.

The variations we find in the accounts of Jesus' life and death in the Gospels fit broadly within the expected parameters of ancient biographies. In Mark and John, nothing is said about Jesus' birth. This is no surprise since ancient biographies did not always include such material. The Gospel stories also often differ on specific details. In Matthew, there is no account of the Holy Family traveling to Bethlehem, while in Luke they go there because of a census. Matthew speaks

---

19 Ibid.

of magi, while Luke's infancy narrative focuses on shepherds. And so on and so forth.

How the details of the different Gospel narratives fit together is not always clear. Still, to conclude from such difficulties that the entire Jesus story is fictional goes too far. The early believers did not think Jesus was a myth. In 2 Peter, we are told, "For we did not follow cleverly concocted *myths* [Greek *mythois*] when we made known to you the power and coming of our Lord Jesus Christ, but we were eyewitnesses of his majesty" (2 Peter 1:16).

Inventing "Fulfillment"?

Some make the specific charge that the New Testament accounts of Jesus' birth should be seen as total inventions because they portray Jesus as fulfilling the Scriptures. Why is Mary depicted as the virgin mother of Jesus? According to some, the story was invented to show that Jesus fulfills Isaiah's Immanuel prophecy. Matthew and Luke, it is said, had to come up with a story that showed that he had been conceived by a "virgin." This is unconvincing.

For one thing, while Isaiah's Immanuel prophecy could be connected to messianic hopes, there is no evidence that Jews thought it necessarily meant that the messiah had to be born of a virgin. Matthew and Luke did not have to make up the story of a virgin birth to prove that Jesus is the Messiah. New Testament writers such as Paul never even mention his Virgin Birth.

Other aspects of the Gospel accounts of Jesus' nativity also point away from the idea that they were wholly made up on the basis of Old Testament prophecies. When Matthew says certain aspects of the Jesus story occurred to "fulfill" the Scriptures, it does not look like he has created his narrative to fit the Old Testament passages he quotes. Matthew's account of Herod's massacre of the infants in Bethlehem is a case in point. In relating the episode, Matthew cites Scripture:

> Then was fulfilled what was said by Jeremiah the prophet: "A voice was heard in Ramah, weeping and great lamentation, Rachel weeping for her children, and she would not be comforted because they are not." (Matthew 2:17–18, citing Jeremiah 31:15)

In context, the passage Matthew quotes *has nothing to do with the Messiah.* Rather, it describes the exile of the Jews into Babylon, which took place in 587 B.C. Matthew's point, as we have seen, is that Israel's story is "summed up" in Jesus' life. Matthew's narrative is certainly shaped by Israel's Scriptures. But Matthew did not have to tell a story of children slaughtered in Bethlehem in order to show that Jeremiah's prophecy had been "fulfilled."

We should not adopt a fundamentalist perspective and insist that the Gospel writers saw themselves recording events as modern historians report them. As we have seen, ancient biographers had different standards than modern historians. Nevertheless, to insist that the story of Jesus is wholly mythological is also unwarranted.

The Word Became Flesh

In the ancient formula known as the Apostles' Creed, Christians have long asserted their conviction that Jesus Christ "suffered under Pontius Pilate." At first, it may seem strange that, of all people, Pilate appears in this ancient summary of the Church's faith. Peter is never mentioned. There is no reference to Paul either. How then does Pontius Pilate rate Creed-worthy?

The Church includes Pilate in the Creed for the same reason Matthew and Luke mention that Jesus was born during the reigns of Augustus Caesar and Herod—the Gospels' accounts about Jesus are set within history. In Christ, the Church recognizes the coming of "God with us." For Christian faith, Jesus is not simply a metaphor or a symbol. It is understood that the world cannot be saved by a mere idea; salvation is found in a *Person.*

Moreover, the reality of Jesus' presence is not just understood to be in the past. Christian tradition maintains that Christ remains "God with us" in the Church's life and worship. This point is made by the English lyrics of "Let All Mortal Flesh Keep Silence." The words of the second verse beautifully express the idea that the eucharistic celebration makes present the mystery of Christ's Incarnation:

> King of kings, yet born of Mary,
> As of old on earth He stood,
> Lord of lords, in human vesture,
> In the body and the blood;
> He will give to all the faithful
> His own self for heav'nly food.

"As of old on earth He stood," Christ is now present in "the body and the blood," which is made our "heav'nly food."

11

"The First Nowell": How December 25 Became Christmas

The exact origins of the song "The First Nowell" are lost to us. Although its title is sometimes spelled with the word *Noël*, the French term for Christmas, the song was likely first written in English. Nevertheless, the English "Nowell" is itself derived from the French word, so the meaning is the same: Christ's birth is the "first Christmas."

As we have seen, however, Jesus' birth is *not* the "first Christmas." "Christmas"—"Christ's mass"—refers *to the celebration of Jesus' nativity*. Nonetheless, as we have discussed, Christian tradition understands that, in the Church's celebration of Christmas, the mystery of Christ's nativity is once again made present.

But when *was* Jesus born?

The earliest Christians did not pass down a unanimous tradition about when Jesus' nativity took place. The first source to give possible dates for Jesus' birth is Clement of Alexandria (A.D. 150–215), who uses the ancient Egyptian calendar. Although he takes no position on the matter himself, he lists various dates he has heard suggested by others.[1] Significantly, he does not indicate that anyone believed Jesus was born on the equivalent of December 25.

---

1   Clement of Alexandria, *Stromateis* 1.21.

One of the dates Clement does mention can be translated to January 6.[2] He does not say, however, that people thought Jesus was born on this day. Rather, he reports that a group of heretics celebrated Jesus' baptism on January 6. Some speculate that these heretics may have believed Jesus was also born on January 6, though that is far from certain.

Either way, that Clement mentions January 6 is notable. We know that some Christians came to see this day as the anniversary of Jesus' birth. Egeria, a pilgrim who visited Jerusalem in the 300s, reports that Jerusalem Christians in her day were honoring the nativity on that date.[3] Notably, Epiphanius, a bishop from Cyprus, also assigns Jesus' birth to this day in the late 300s.[4] The Armenian Orthodox Church still marks it as the feast of Jesus' birth.

It is worth noting here that Eastern Orthodox Christians celebrate Christmas on January 7. This is because these Christians follow the old Julian calendar (named after Julius Caesar). The Julian calendar was in use from 46 B.C. until the 1500s, when Pope Gregory XVI introduced a new calendar— the "Gregorian calendar"—that uses a more precise system of leap years. Today, virtually all countries use the Gregorian calendar. Many non-Catholic religious groups, however, still mark holy days by using the old Julian calendar. Eastern Orthodox Christians, therefore, still celebrate Christmas on a "December 25," but it is the December 25 of the old Julian calendar, which corresponds to our January 7—that is, January 7 on the Gregorian calendar.

How then did December 25 become Christmas? Some believe it can be deduced from details in Luke's narrative. Others believe it was in response to a pagan festival. Still others

---

2   See Susan K. Roll, *Toward the Origins of Christmas* (Kampen, Netherlands: Kok Pharos Publishing House, 1995), 77–79.

3   Egeria, *Pilgrimage* 25–26.

4   Epiphanius, *Panarion* 51.24.1.

believe that December 25 came to be the feast of the Nativity due to early Christian chronological calculations. Here we will consider the evidence.

The Time of Jesus' Birth in the Gospel of Luke

Some people make the case that we can figure out or narrow down the time of year Jesus was born by analyzing details in the New Testament accounts. Two elements in the Gospel of Luke are often singled out as significant: (1) the fact that shepherds were in the field on the night of the nativity (Luke 2:8) and (2) the details surrounding Gabriel's announcement of John the Baptist's birth to Zechariah, which Luke places six months before the Annunciation to Mary (Luke 1:24, 26, 36).

The Shepherds in the Field

Many have insisted that since Luke has shepherds out in the field on the night of Jesus' birth (Luke 2:8), Christ could not have been born in winter. This assertion rests on evidence from later Jewish sources that place the grazing period for sheep between April and November.[5] Yet since these sources are dated centuries after the time of Jesus, their historical reliability on such matters is questionable. Furthermore, an earlier report from the Mishnah, a second-century source, seems to point in a different direction. It implies that Passover lambs grazed in February, one of the coldest months of the year.[6] If that is the case, there is no reason to think shepherds could not have been in the field in the winter (though we should not

---

5 Babylonian Talmud, Betzah 40a; Jerusalem Talmud, Betzah 63b.
6 Mishnah Sheqalim 7.4.

conclude that the shepherds in Luke were necessarily watching over the lambs sacrificed at Passover). Furthermore, we cannot rule out the possibility of an unusually warm winter. All things being equal, the account of the shepherds' location does seem to make a winter date less likely. Still, we should not hang too much on this detail.

Calculations Based on Zechariah's Supposed High Priesthood

Some ancient writers attempted to prove that December 25 was the correct date of Jesus' birth based on the idea that Gabriel appeared to Zechariah on the feast of the Day of Atonement. The earliest advocate of this position seems to be John Chrysostom, who preached a homily on the date of Christmas in A.D. 386.[7] According to Chrysostom, Zechariah was the high priest. When Gabriel appeared to him, he was performing the temple rites of the Day of Atonement. Since this feast takes place in the fall, Chrysostom placed the scene of the annunciation to Zechariah in September. Luke informs us that Gabriel's announcement to Mary took place six months later (Luke 1:24, 26, 36). This, Chrysostom argues, means Mary must have conceived Jesus in March and, therefore, given birth in December, nine months later. Chrysostom's argument, however, is based on a faulty assumption. As we have seen, Zechariah was not the high priest, and Luke's account of Gabriel's visit to him is not said to be on the Day of Atonement. Instead, Zechariah is simply performing the rites of the daily *Tamid* offering.

Here we may detect the influence of the popular work known as the *Protoevangelium of James*, written in the late

---

7   John Chrysostom's Christmas homily can be found in *Patrologia Graeca* 49:351–62.

100s, which makes Zechariah out to be the high priest. Its portrait of Zechariah serving in the temple at the time of the Day of Atonement should not be seen as reflecting ancient Christian memory about the timing of John's and Jesus' births. Rather, its depiction results from a misinterpretation of Luke's narrative.

Calculations Based on Zechariah's Priestly Service

Before moving on, another attempt to calculate the timing of Jesus' birth from Luke should also be mentioned. More recent writers have argued that we can determine the time of year Zechariah had his encounter with Gabriel by zeroing in on the fact that Zechariah is said to be from the priestly line of Abijah (Luke 1:5). For example, German writer Josef Heinrich Friedlieb argued in 1887 that the line of Abijah served in the temple in September.[8] Following Luke's timeline of events like Chrysostom did, he argued that this would put the conception of Jesus in March and his birth in December. The problem here is that the first plank in the argument fails: Friedlieb's case that Zechariah's priestly division served in the temple in September is chock-full of problems. Those who follow him are simply ignorant of the issues that undermine his argument.

First, proposals such as Friedlieb's rely on later Jewish works such as the Babylonian Talmud, which contain errors about first-century Jewish practice. It is true that the Dead Sea Scrolls, which date to Jesus' day, also mention the priestly courses.[9] Nevertheless, the data they provide is insufficient to

---

8   Josef Heinrich Friedlieb, *Leben J. Christi des Erlösers* (Münster: Druck und Verlag von Ferdinand Schöningh, 1887), 312.

9   4QCalendrical Document A.

reconstruct what was happening year by year in the Jerusalem temple.

Second, even if we *could* reconstruct the cycles of the priestly courses in the first century, we cannot assume that they ran without interruptions or variations. Ancient Jews had to deal with the problem of "intercalation"; that is, they had to reconcile the 365-day solar year with the 354-day lunar calendar. They did not have our regular system of "leap years." Second-century rabbis tell us that the authorities would, at times, add an extra month to the calendar,[10] but we do not know how and when this occurred.[11] Suffice it to say, this is a *massive* problem that affects the whole matter under discussion here. What "should" have been a given date according to the cycle of the moon may not have been. We therefore have no way to know how the priestly divisions rotated in any given year. In sum, we cannot determine when Zechariah was serving in the temple based on Luke's narrative.

How then did Christians choose December 25 as the feast of Jesus' birth? Scholars have generally taken one of two approaches: (1) the History of Religions Theory, which basically holds that December 25 was chosen to counter a pagan holy day, and (2) the Calculation Theory, which holds that the date emerged from a complex process of Christian computations. We will first consider the History of Religions Theory before turning our attention to look at how early Christians tried to calculate the time of Jesus' birth.

Christmas and Paganism

Was December 25 first a pagan holiday? For some, this notion would seem to discredit Christianity. Here we will consider

---

10   Mishnah Eduyyot 7.7.
11   Stéphane Saulnier, *Calendrical Variations in Second Temple Judaism: New Perspectives on the "Date of the Last Supper" Debate* (Leiden: Brill, 2012), 274.

the standard versions of the History of Religions Theory of the origins of Christmas.

Sanctifying Pagan Culture

In the last chapter, we examined the claims of mythicists who believe that Jesus is not a historical figure. Many of them advance a version of the History of Religions Theory regarding December 25. According to them, Jesus is said to have been born on December 25 because other gods were said to be born on this day. In their minds, the choice to mark the nativity of Jesus on December 25 somehow proves that Jesus was never a historical figure. Yet their logic does not follow.

Historical evidence for Jesus' existence long predates the earliest source identifying December 25 as Jesus' birth. Whatever associations it had for pagans, the later decision to honor Jesus' birth on this date cannot somehow be used as proof against Jesus' historical existence.

From the standpoint of the Christian faith, there would be nothing intrinsically objectionable about choosing to remember Christ's birth on a day important to pagans. The Old Testament uses names for the God of Israel—for example, "El" (Job 36:26; Psalm 102:25)—that were originally used for pagan gods.[12] By using these divine names, the Bible does not endorse paganism. Instead, by using such appellations for the Lord, the Scriptures make a profound statement: the God of Israel is the one Creator to whom all other so-called gods—sometimes described as demons (Deuteronomy 32:17)—are subject.

Similar kinds of cultural adaptations can be found in later Christian tradition as well. For example, Christians came to

---

12 See John Day, *YHWH and the Gods and Goddesses of Canaan*, Journal for the Study of the Old Testament Supplement Series 265 (Sheffield: Sheffield Academic Press, 2002).

use wedding rings as sacramental symbols. The practice does not seem to have been widespread in ancient Israel but, rather, appears to be derived from Greco-Roman culture. For Christians, finger rings became a sign of a couple's commitment to one another in Christ.[13] Yet it was certainly not an endorsement of paganism.

According to Justin Martyr, there were "seeds of truth" found in pagan writers. While they did not "grasp their exact meaning," these writers pointed forward to the truth of the Gospel.[14] Likewise, John Henry Newman, the great theologian and scholar from the late 1800s, speaks of how the Church has "sanctified" elements from pagan culture:

> Incense, lamps, and candles; votive offerings on recovery from illness; holy water; asylums; holy days and seasons, use of calendars, processions, blessings on the fields; sacerdotal vestments, the tonsure, the ring in marriage ... are all of pagan origin, and sanctified by their adoption into the Church.[15]

Newman would go on to insist that elements adapted from pagan cultures need to be purified; they should not be embraced uncritically. Nonetheless, adaptation of pagan practices or customs is not itself foreign to Christian tradition. The "inculturation" of the Gospel has long been recognized as part of the Church's mission. To proclaim the message of Christ, Christian missionaries have appealed to familiar symbols and customs. Nevertheless, the standard accounts of the History of Religions Theory of how December 25 became Christmas are unpersuasive.

---

13 Tertullian, *Apology* 6.3; Susan Treggiari, *Roman Marriage: Iusti Coniuges from the Time of Cicero to the Time of Ulpian* (Oxford: Clarendon Press, 1991), 148–50.
14 Justin Martyr, *First Apology* 44.
15 John Henry Newman, *An Essay on the Development of Christian Doctrine* (London: James Toovey, 1845), 359–60.

The Roman Festival of Saturnalia and Christmas

Many have placed the origins of Christmas in the Roman festival of Saturnalia, which was dedicated to the god Saturn. The festival was associated with feasting and merriment. During the week-long celebration, civil norms were upended. For example, masters would serve their slaves at table. But it certainly went beyond innocent fun. The feast was also associated with immoral excess. The ancient writer Macrobius reports—probably with some exaggeration—that during the festival "every kind of license is permitted to the slaves."[16]

Yet the problem with identifying Saturnalia as the origin for Christmas is that their dates do not line up. Saturnalia ran from December 17 to December 23—*not* December 25! The Saturnalia celebration, therefore, cannot explain how December 25 became the feast of Christ's nativity.

The Feast of the Unconquered Sun

A second History of Religions approach focuses specifically on December 25. According to this explanation, the day was chosen to mark Jesus' birth because Romans worshipped a sun god on this date. The Roman emperor Aurelian, it is said, promoted the worship of a god known as *Sol Invictus*, the "Unconquered Sun," in A.D. 274. Aurelian, the story goes, made December 25 "the day of the birth of the Unconquered Sun."

Yet the notion that Christians chose to celebrate the birth of Jesus because of the feast of *Sol Invictus* is increasingly questioned by scholars. For one thing, the first historical source that confirms that a pagan god was worshipped on

16 *Saturnalia* 1.7.26.

December 25 is called the *Chronograph*, which was compiled in A.D. 336. Here the entry for December 25 reads: "Birthday of Invictus." "Invictus" is likely a reference to the sun god. This day was celebrated with chariot races. We therefore have no hard evidence that December 25 was connected to a sun god until the *Chronograph*, which dates to long after the death of Aurelian in A.D. 275. In fact, scholars are now showing that the case for the popularity of the sun god *Sol Invictus* seems to be based more on the imaginations of writers from the 1800s than in verifiable historical sources.[17]

Remarkably, the *Chronograph* also contains the earliest uncontestable reference to the fact that Christians celebrated Christmas on December 25. It reads, "December 25, Christ is born in Bethlehem of Judea."[18] Therefore, while many have assumed that December 25 was first chosen by the worshippers of *Sol Invictus*, there is no proof of this. Perhaps December 25 was *first* a Christian holy day.

But how and when did Christians come to this date? We now turn to the Calculation Theory.

Ancient Attempts to Date Jesus' Birth

Advocates of the Calculation Theory argue that early Christians decided on marking the nativity of Jesus on December 25 due to complex chronological computations. There is clear evidence that supports this explanation; some certainly did this. However, as we shall see, this does not fully make sense of why December 25 was selected as the date of Christ's nativity.

---

17   Steven Hijmans, "Usener's *Christmas*," in *Hermann Usener und die Metamorphosen der Philologie*, ed. Michel Espagne and Pascale Rabault-Feuerhahn (Wiesbaden: Harrassowitz, 2011): 139–51.

18   Translation from Thomas C. Schmidt, "Calculating December 25 as the Birth of Jesus in Hippolytus' *Canon* and *Chronicon*," *Vigiliae Christianae* 69 (2015): 543.

Jewish Traditions about the Births of Biblical Persons

It is often said that early Christians were influenced by a Jewish tradition that held that the great figures of Israel's past died on the day of their birth. This is sometimes called the "integral age" view. Evidence for this tradition can be found in the Babylonian Talmud, which dates to around A.D. 500. For example, the Talmud claims that Moses died on the anniversary of his birth.[19] It also reports opinions about the birth and death of Abraham and Jacob.[20] While they disagree on the exact month, the rabbis agree that these patriarchs were born and died on the same month the world was created, though they are never said to have died on their birthdays. One teacher coordinates their births and deaths with the month Passover is celebrated. At another point, we are told that another patriarch, Isaac, was born on Passover.

By dying on the anniversary of their births, these men are said to have lived "the full measure" of their years. In connection with this, the Talmud cites the Scripture passage: "I will fulfill the number of your days" (Exodus 23:26). Many writers have believed that early Christians were influenced by these Jewish traditions and applied them to Jesus. This, however, is unclear. The Talmud dates to hundreds of years after the period we are examining. Whether Christians who were trying to determine the date of Jesus' birth were influenced by the Jewish traditions described above is impossible to know.

Nevertheless, there are some parallels between what the rabbis said about the patriarchs and what is found in ancient Christian chronologists. For one thing, it does seem like calculations regarding Jesus' conception or birth were connected to beliefs about when his death occurred. In fact, early Christians

---

19 Qiddushin 38a.
20 Babylonian Talmud Rosh Hashanah 10b–11a.

had some important data about the time of year Jesus died to work from as a starting point.

Early Christian Calculations

When it comes to the date of Jesus' death, the Gospels provided early Christian chronologists a few parameters. First, according to the New Testament writers, Jesus was crucified during the week of Passover (Matthew 26:17–19; Mark 14:12–16; Luke 22:7–13; John 13:1–2).[21] That feast always occurs during the spring. Furthermore, the Law of Moses stipulates that Passover must occur on the fifteenth day of the Jewish month of Nisan (Exodus 12:6). This meant the feast had to coincide with a full moon. Second, Jesus died the day before the Sabbath—that is, on a Friday (Mark 15:42; Luke 23:54; John 19:31). Third, since Jesus' ministry began during the fifteenth year of Caesar Tiberius (Luke 3:1), his death had to fall within a few years of that period. Based on all of this information and using complex computations based on the cycles of the moon, some early Christians sought to identify the precise date of Christ's Passion.

The earliest Christian chronology known to us was written by the third-century writer Julius Africanus. It was entitled the *Chronographiae,* and it can be dated to A.D. 221. The original text is lost to us, but it is cited and quoted by later writers. Scholars have attempted to piece it back together based on these other sources.[22] It is generally agreed that Africanus dated Jesus' Resurrection to March 25, A.D. 31.[23] What is

---

21 On the apparent tension between the Synoptic and Johannine chronologies of the Passion, see Brant Pitre, *Jesus and the Last Supper* (Grand Rapids, MI: Eerdmans, 2015), 251–373.

22 Martin Wallraff, ed., *Iulius Africanus Chronographiae: The Extant Fragments*, trans. William Adler (Berlin: Walter de Gruyter, 2007).

23 Alden A. Mosshammer, *The Easter Computus and the Origins of the Christian Era* (Oxford: Oxford University Press, 2008), 406–7.

more, Africanus also seems to have placed Jesus' conception on March 25, the date he believed marked the creation of the sun. If this is correct, there is good reason to think that he placed Jesus' birth in December—that is, nine months after Africanus thought he had been conceived.[24]

In Africanus' conclusions we can detect some similarities with the Jewish traditions mentioned from the Babylonian Talmud above, though differences are also present. As the rabbis believed Moses was born and died in the same month, for Africanus Jesus' conception (but not his birth) is correlated with the date of his Resurrection (not his death). Moreover, as the Talmud connects Abraham's and Jacob's births and deaths to the month of Creation, Africanus ties Jesus' conception and Resurrection to Creation.

Complications in Calculations

Yet calculating Jesus' birth was not a straightforward process. We know that those who made such computations ran into problems and tensions. This is evident in two early chronological works, the *Canon* and the *Chronicon*, which are traditionally attributed to Hippolytus, an early Christian theologian. Even if he is not their actual author, there is good reason to think they came from the same hand.[25] The *Canon* and the *Chronicon* rely on calculations that chart out the cycles of the moon. Based on these lunar tables, they offer a timeline of events going all the way back to Creation. A fragment

---

24 See C. Philipp E. Nothaft, "Early Christian Chronology and the Origins of the Christmas Date: In Defense of the 'Calculation Theory,'" *Questions liturgiques* 94 (2013): 247–65, esp. 262–64.

25 For discussion and sources, see Schmidt, "Calculating December 25," 546–47; T. C. Schmidt, *Hippolytus of Rome: Commentary on Daniel and 'Chronicon'* (Piscataway, NJ: Gorgias Press, 2017). The *Canon* should not be confused with the so-called *Canons of Hippolytus*, which contain thirty-eight decrees that are falsely attributed to him.

of the *Canon* was found inscribed on a statue in Rome. The inscription dates to A.D. 222.

The *Canon* concludes that Jesus died on March 25 of the year 29. Tertullian, another second-century Christian writer, also fixes the Crucifixion to this date.[26] This agreement suggests that the date had found acceptance by at least some Christians.

Given that it fixes Jesus' death to March 25, it is important to point out that the *Canon* indicates that Jesus' "genesis" (Greek: *genesis*) occurred on April 2 of 2 B.C. While this may be taken as a reference to his birth, it could refer instead to his conception.[27] Either way, this data is significant. It shows that ancient Christians did not always feel the need to correlate the date of Jesus' conception or birth with that of his death or Resurrection. So why April 2? According to the timetables used by the *Canon*, April 2 of 2 B.C. fell during a Passover week. Thus, like later Jewish traditions about the patriarchs, the *Chronicon* seeks to tie Jesus' human beginnings to a Passover backdrop.

There is a further piece of data that should be considered. A commentary on Daniel that is attributed to Hippolytus assigns Jesus' birth to December 25.[28] Its authorship is debated, but some believe it was written by the same person who wrote the *Canon* and the *Chronicon*.[29] If the commentary did originally state that Jesus was born on December 25, it would be our earliest source dating Jesus' birth to that day. This, however, is debated.

The December 25 date appears in five of the six manuscripts of the Daniel commentary, including our earliest copy. In one version, however, two dates are given: April 2 and December 25. Some believe April 2 represents the original date for Jesus' birth and that the reference to December 25 was therefore

---

26 Tertullian, *Against the Jews* 8.18.
27 Schmidt, "Calculating December 25," 547–52.
28 Hippolytus, *On Daniel* 4.23.3.
29 Mosshammer, *Easter Computus*, 121.

inserted into the document by a later writer after the feast of the Nativity came to be celebrated in December. Yet it is just as possible that the April 2 date refers to Jesus' *conception* and not to his birth. In this scenario, it would not necessarily be a problem that two dates appear. Moreover, if the text did originally say that Jesus was conceived in April and born in December, this might mean that the December date was not arrived at simply because it was believed Jesus was conceived in March. But we have no idea what other factors may have led the author to a December date.

Finally, one last point should be made: the calculations in the *Chronicon* do not always align with the timelines provided in the Bible.[30] For example, in order to show that Jesus was conceived (or born) during the same month God created the world, the *Chronicon* must contradict aspects of both the biblical narrative and the *Canon*. It does not seem to be the case, then, that math was the only factor in the author's choice of certain dates. When we look at the work of ancient chronologists, then, we see that two dates continue to emerge as significant: March 25 and December 25. Africanus thought Jesus was conceived and rose from the dead on March 25. Tertullian thought Jesus died on March 25, a date the *Canon* seems to confirm. Moreover, if Africanus thought Jesus was conceived on March 25, he very likely put his birth nine months later—on December 25, the same day Jesus' birth is assigned to in the Daniel commentary. What was so important about these dates? Their appeal is no mystery.

The Winter Solstice

On the old Roman calendar, March 25 marked the spring equinox, the time of year when day and night are of equal

---

30 For the following, see Schmidt, "Calculating December 25," 29–31.

length. ("Equinox" literally means "equal night.") The same calendar also placed the winter solstice, the time of year when daylight begins to increase, on December 25. Early Christians found great significance in these dates.

The Creation of the Sun and Christ's Conception

Many ancient Christian writers such as Julius Africanus believed that God created the sun on March 25, the spring equinox. Their reasoning was based on Scripture. In Genesis, the reason God makes the heavenly lights—the sun, moon, and stars—is to "separate the day from the night" (Genesis 1:14). It was assumed that when God divided the day and the night, he separated them evenly. Since day and night are evenly divided during the spring equinox, March 25 was believed to be the day God created the sun and the moon. Africanus and others therefore placed the conception of Christ on this day; Jesus' earthly beginnings were therefore connected with that of the sun's.

But why connect Christ and the sun? The association was suggested by the Scriptures.

Various New Testament passages apply sun and light imagery to Jesus. In Luke, Zechariah speaks of Christ's work of redemption as "the dawn from on high" (Luke 1:78). In John, Jesus says, "I am the light of the world" (John 8:12; 9:5; cf. John 1:4–5, 7–9). In the Apocalypse, John has a vision of Jesus, whose face "was like *the sun shining at full strength*" (Revelation 1:16).

The early Christians read the New Testament in the light of the Old Testament. Given the New Testament's application of sun imagery to Jesus, a prophecy from the book of Malachi was seen as pointing to Christ:

> But for you who fear my name *the sun of righteousness* shall rise, with healing in its wings. (Malachi 4:2)

Many of the earliest Christian writers believed the "sun of righteousness" was a reference to Christ.[31] This influenced Christian thinking about when Jesus was conceived.

Furthermore, by connecting the conception of Jesus with the creation of the sun, early Christians were signaling new creation hopes; Jesus' conception marked the beginning of a new creation.

Christmas and the Winter Solstice

It is no surprise, then, that December 25 became a popular date for Jesus' birth. The date worked well with the winter solstice. Jesus, the "sun of righteousness," was understood to be born at the very time sunlight begins to "grow." Just as the equinox in March was a fitting setting for Jesus' conception, so too the winter solstice was seen as an appropriate time to mark Jesus' birth.

Later works would develop the imagery further. If Jesus' conception takes place on March 25, following Luke's timeline, Elizabeth would have conceived John the Baptist six months earlier. John's birth could therefore be tied to June 24, which is the summer solstice. It is at this time of year that the length of days decrease. The symbolism was connected to what John the Baptist says about Jesus: "He must increase, but I must decrease" (John 3:30).

It seems, then, that Christians were drawn to celebrate the nativity on December 25 due to the symbolism that the winter solstice evoked. By celebrating the nativity on this day, Christians were making a statement: the meaning of creation is ultimately found in Christ. Of course, in choosing this date to remember Jesus' birth, Christians made a bold statement: pagan interpretations of the universe are false—Jesus Christ is the true Lord of creation.

---

31 Clement of Alexandria, *Exhortation to the Heathen* 11; Origen, *Homilies on Leviticus* 13.2.1.

By the time of Augustine, the Church's calendar was largely settled. In about A.D. 420, Augustine writes that Jesus "is believed to have been conceived on 25 of March, and also to have suffered on that day.... But tradition has it that he was born on 25 of December."[32]

Jerome, Augustine's contemporary, would argue that the timing of the feasts points to the truth of the Gospel:

> Even nature is in agreement with our claim, for the world itself bears witness to our statement. Up to this day, darkness increases; from this day on, it decreases; light increases, darkness decreases.... For us today, the Sun of Justice is born.[33]

From this time on, the identification of Jesus with the sun would find expression throughout Christian writings and devotions. For example, in the third stanza of the classic Christmas carol "Hark! The Herald Angels Sing" we find the lines: "Hail the heaven-born Prince of Peace! *Hail the Sun of Righteousness!*" Here the song unmistakably applies Malachi's sun prophecy to Christ.

The Challenge of December 25

Yet the adoption of December 25 would not come without problems. Some pagan converts seem to have retained certain superstitions associated with sun worship. In the mid-400s, Leo the Great speaks about those who still pay homage to the rising sun at the top of the steps of St. Peter's Basilica.

---

32 Augustine, *On the Trinity* 4.2.9, trans. Edmund Hill (Hyde Park: New City Press, 1991), 159.
33 Jerome, *Homily* 88, trans. Sr. Marie Ligouri Ewald, in *The Homilies of Saint Jerome (Homilies 60–96)* (Washington, DC: Catholic University of America Press, 1966), 226–27.

> Before entering the blessed Apostle Peter's basilica ... when
> they have mounted the steps ... they turn round and bow
> themselves towards the rising sun and with bent neck do
> homage to its brilliant orb. We are full of grief and vexation
> that this should happen.[34]

By putting the feast of the Nativity on a date of cosmic importance, Christianity would be making a bold assertion: creation
points to Christ. But this would also lead to misunderstand-
ings. In another sermon, Leo himself says:

> Simple minds are deceived by some who hold the pernicious
> belief that our celebration today seems to derive its high posi-
> tion, not from the birth of Christ, but from, as they say, the
> rising of the "new sun." The hearts of these people are envel-
> oped in enormous shadows and they are ... still seduced by
> the most stupid pagan errors.[35]

The Church did not likely choose December 25 simply to
counter the worship of *Sol Invictus*. The best evidence suggests
that the pieces for the December 25 birthdate of Jesus were
already in place by the end of the 200s, long before there is
evidence that a feast honoring a pagan sun god took place on
this date. Nevertheless, the symbolism of the winter solstice
was certainly open to being misconstrued.

By celebrating the nativity in proximity to the winter solstice, Christians were able to highlight the way Jesus fulfills
the meaning of the cosmos. In this, we see that while the Calculation Theory rests on strong evidence, aspects of the History of Religion Theory remain relevant. The two approaches
are not entirely incompatible. The cosmic symbolism of the

---

34 Leo the Great, *Sermon* 22.6, in *Nicene and Post-Nicene Fathers: Second Series*, 12:140.
35 Leo the Great, *Sermon* 27.4, in Roll, *Toward Origins of Christmas*, 154.

March equinox and December solstice made March 25 and December 25 extremely appealing.

Still, by choosing December 25, the Church was selecting a date that could very easily be misconstrued. Many Christians today often bemoan the "war" on Christmas. The truth is, the Church fired the first volley. By celebrating Christ's birth on December 25, Christians proclaimed that the world's story is ultimately summed up in Christ.

What is surprising, however, was that after the rise of Christianity, it was certain self-professed Christians who led the charge to ban the December 25 celebration of Jesus' nativity. How did that take place? The story—and the lessons we can learn from it—is the subject of our final chapter. As we shall see, the modern Christmas celebration, including the prominence of Santa Claus and Christmas trees, is deeply anchored in religious symbolism.

12

"It's Beginning to Look a Lot Like Christmas": The Development of the Christmas Celebration

The song "It's Beginning to Look a Lot Like Christmas," written in 1951 by Meredith Wilson, tells us what the Christmas season is "supposed" to look like:

> It's beginning to look a lot like Christmas
> Everywhere you go;
> Take a look at the five and ten, it's glistening once again
> With candy canes and silver lanes that glow.

Later lines describe "a tree in the grand hotel" and "the holly that will be on your own front door."

It should go without saying that the ancient Christians would have recognized few of the things mentioned in Wilson's song. Christmas trees and other such decorations are certainly not described in Scripture. Does this mean that they are incompatible with the Bible's message? Where did Christmas trees come from? And how did Saint Nicholas become "Santa Claus"? No Christmas book would be complete without a discussion of these things. Here, then, we offer an overview of the history of Christmas—and the important lessons we can learn from the story.

Christmas as a Season

Many Christians dislike the greeting "happy holidays" because they suspect it is meant to slight the religious meaning
of Christmas. What is often forgotten is that the term "holiday" is derived from the term "holy day." Whatever the intent
behind it, "happy holidays" is not *intrinsically* inappropriate
for Christians. It reflects an ancient idea—namely, that *Christmas is constituted by a series of holy days rather than referring
to a single holy day.* As we shall see, the notion of a "Christmas
season" developed soon after Christmas was fixed on December 25.

The Holy Days of Christmas Season

As I mentioned at the beginning of the previous chapter,
before the practice of celebrating Jesus' birth on December 25
became widely adopted, many early Christians celebrated it on
January 6. The decision to mark the nativity on December 25,
however, meant that January 6 could become more focused
on the visit of the magi. January 6 would eventually become
known as the Epiphany (the "manifestation") of Jesus. It
developed into a major feast of its own and was also associated
with Jesus' baptism and his first miracle at the Wedding Feast
at Cana (John 2:1–11). January 6 is even sometimes referred
to as "Little Christmas."

Between December 25 and January 1, several other important feasts were fixed. The Council of Ephesus defined Mary as
the "Mother of God" in A.D. 431. This title was not meant to
indicate that Mary is some sort of "goddess" or anything like
that. Rather, the title was about preserving the truth of Jesus'
identity as God; he is not just the Messiah but the Lord.

After this, Roman Christians began to mark Mary's maternity on January 1. In Spain and France, however, the day became associated with the circumcision of Jesus, which Luke tells us took place on his eighth day, in accord with the Torah (Luke 2:21).

Since there were eight days between December 25 and January 1, it was natural to celebrate Christmas as an "octave." The notion has biblical roots. The Law of Moses stipulates that the Feast of Tabernacles is to last eight days (Leviticus 23:36). Since Easter was also celebrated with an octave, it was natural to do the same for the feast of Christ's nativity.

Moreover, the three days after December 25 became important feasts in their own right. On December 26, the Church celebrated Saint Stephen, whose martyrdom is described in the book of Acts (Acts 7:54–60). John the Apostle was honored on December 27. Finally, the "Holy Innocents"—that is, the children massacred by Herod (Matthew 2:16)—were remembered on December 28. The connection between these feasts and Christmas was not hard to explain. The ancient Christians saw the deaths of saints as marking their "birthdays" into eternal life. Notably, in the *Chronograph*, the reference to Jesus' birth immediately proceeds a list of martyrs' names with their "birthdays." The oldest indisputable source identifying December 25 as the feast of Jesus' birth, therefore, ties it to the concept of martyrdom. Moreover, the combination of Stephen, John the Apostle, and the Holy Innocents came to be seen as significant for another reason.

Although there is some conflicting testimony, John the Apostle became especially remembered for dying a natural death. According to tradition, this only happened after he survived attempts to execute him. Tertullian, for example, reports that John miraculously survived being put in a vat of burning oil.[1] Another story recounts how John drank poison and lived.[2]

Over time, then, a rationale emerged for the Church's remembrance of the Apostle John and the Holy Innocents together with Stephen. Jacob of Voragine, a medieval writer, put it this way:

> There are three kinds of martyrdom: the first is willed and endured, the second is willed but not endured, the third endured without being willed. Saint Stephen is an example of the first, Saint John of the second, and the Holy Innocents of the third.[3]

In other words, Stephen represents those who spill their blood for the faith, John symbolizes those who are willing to offer themselves for Christ but who nonetheless die of some other cause, and the innocent children from Bethlehem are a reminder of those who give their lives for Christ without knowing it. As the Church contemplates the "birthday" of Jesus, Christians also reflect on the various ways the saints experience their birthdays into eternal life.

The Twelve and Forty Days of Christmas

Between Christmas Day on December 25 and the Epiphany on January 6 there are twelve days. The Church in France,

---

1 Tertullian, *Prescription against Heresies* 36.
2 *Acts of the Holy Apostle and Evangelist John the Theologians*, in *Ante-Nicene Fathers*, 8:560–62. See also Sean McDowell, *The Fate of the Twelve Apostles: Examining the Martyrdom Accounts of the Closest Followers of Jesus* (Farnham, UK: Ashgate Publishing, 2015), 152–56.
3 Jacob of Voragine, *The Golden Legend*, trans. William Granger Ryan, 2 vols. (Princeton, NJ: Princeton University Press, 1993), 1:50.

therefore, began to emphasize this time frame as significant. Today it is especially known because of the popular song "The Twelve Days of Christmas." The song refers to two turtle-doves, which is the sacrifice offered by the Holy Family after Jesus' birth in Luke (Luke 2:24). This has prompted many to believe that the other verses in the song also have spiritual significance. Some have even claimed the song's coded imagery was invented by English Catholics who used the lyrics to teach the faith secretly during times of persecution. There is no historical evidence, however, to support this theory. Still, the song has helpfully popularized the notion that Christmas is a *season*, rather than a single day.

Finally, a Christmas-themed feast occurs after the Epiphany on January 6. Luke tells us that the Holy Family came to the temple forty days after Jesus' birth to offer sacrifice in the temple. The Church began to celebrate the Holy Family's trip to the temple on February 2, forty days after December 25. In the Gospel of Luke, the episode includes a declaration from the elderly man Simeon that Christ has come as a "light" to the Gentiles (Luke 2:32). It therefore became a tradition to distribute blessed candles to the faithful on this day. As a result, it became known as "Candlemas." While not technically part of the Church's liturgical season of Christmas, the celebration of the Holy Family's visit to the temple can be considered part of the Christmas cycle since it closes out a series of feast days relating to Christ's infancy.

Celebrating Christmas among the Ancient Pagans

From ancient times, Christians marked the feast of the Nativity while the world around them celebrated other winter festivals. This presented challenges.

Christmas and Pagan Winter Celebrations

As we have seen, by choosing December 25, the Church chose to commemorate the birth of Jesus during a time of year that was already associated with feasting and celebration. From December 17 to 23, Rome was immersed in the festivities of Saturnalia. In addition, ancient Romans marked New Year's Day on January 1 with presents and partying. Christian preachers would warn their flocks against participating in such celebrations, which were characterized by drunkenness and pagan superstitions.

For example, Augustine contrasts the pagans' conduct on New Year's Day with the self-discipline and charitable activities of the Church:

> They give New Year's presents: you give alms! They entertain themselves with debauched singing: find your entertainment in the words of the Scriptures! They run to the theater:[4] you go to church! They get drunk: you practice fasting! If you cannot fast today, at least eat with moderation.[5]

Augustine goes on to say that Christians who participate in pagan New Year's celebrations, which were associated with the pagan god Janus, are "taking incense from their hearts and placing it before devils."

Yule and Christmas

Yet there was also a recognition that pagan culture needed to be "baptized." At the end of the 500s, we encounter another

---

4 Theatrical productions often involved immoral and salacious portrayals.

5 Augustine, *Sermon* 17, trans. Thomas Comerford Lawler, in *St. Augustine: Sermons for Christmas and Epiphany* (Mahwah, NJ: Newman Press, 1952), 151; slightly adapted.

Augustine who is now remembered as "Augustine of Canterbury" (to distinguish him from the great bishop from Hippo quoted above). This later Augustine was a monk. However, he would not be allowed to remain in seclusion from the world. Gregory the Great chose him to become the great missionary to the Anglo-Saxons in the southeast of England.

The English historian Bede reports that Gregory gave Augustine of Canterbury the following advice on how to help pagan converts embrace Christianity. The quotation is lengthy but important to read as it reveals Gregory's insight into the practicalities of spreading the Gospel:

> The temples of the idols in that nation should by no means be destroyed, but only the idols in them. Take holy water and sprinkle it in these shrines, build altars and place relics in them. For if the shrines are well built, it is essential that they be converted from the worship of devils to the service of the true God. When this people see that their temples are not destroyed they will be able to banish error from their hearts and be more ready to come to the places they are familiar with, but now recognizing and worshipping the true God.... It is doubtless impossible to cut out everything at once from their stubborn minds: just as the man who is attempting to climb to the highest place, rises by steps and degrees and not by leaps.[6]

Many believe Gregory's strategy of adapting pagan customs had implications for Christmas. Christian missionaries could infuse practices associated with pagan winter festivals with Christian meaning. The extent of this adaptation, however, is unclear.

---

6   Gregory the Great, *Ecclesiastical History of the English People* 1.30, trans. Judith McClure and Roger Collins (Oxford: Oxford University Press, 1969); slightly adapted.

For instance, it is believed that northern Europeans celebrated a pagan religious feast called "Yule," which involved
sumptuous feasts. Many believe certain Christmas traditions
have origins in this festival. Perhaps the best known is the
practice of selecting and burning a log (a "Yule Log").

Writers in the 1800s, especially German ones, highlighted the supposed connections between Christmas celebrations and earlier pre-Christian observances. The reason this
approach was appealing was that it promoted nationalistic
pride. However, our knowledge of pre-Christian pagan practices in places like northern Europe is murky. These societies
were often illiterate, and so ancient historical documentation
about their customs is unavailable to us. It is therefore hard
to know how much real influence these pagan practices had
on the Christmas celebration. Scholars, therefore, now express
more caution about approaches that seek to root Christmas
traditions in these pagan festivals.[7] Regardless, these explanations have captured popular imagination and continue to be
advanced today. The term "Yule" has therefore now become
synonymous with Christmas. For instance, the familiar carol
"Deck the Halls" includes the line "Troll the ancient *yuletide*
carol." In this context, to "troll" means to sing with a full,
rolling voice. Singing a "yuletide" hymn, therefore, now refers
to singing a Christmas carol.

The War on Christmas

For most of Christian history, the notion of keeping Christmas was not controversial. What many might find surprising, however, is that the first salvo in the so-called "war on

---

7   See Joe Perry, "Germany and Scandinavia," in *The Oxford Handbook of Christmas*, ed. Timothy Larsen (Oxford: Oxford University Press, 2020), 446–47.

Christmas" was fired not from nonreligious objectors to Christ's nativity but from Christians. In fact, as we shall see, the present-day shape of the Christmas celebration is inexplicable without this past.

The Puritans' Objections to Christmas

The initial leader of the Protestant Reformation, Martin Luther, not only approved of observing the nativity of Jesus on December 25, but even wrote hymns and sermons devoted to it. His fondness for Christmas was so well known that some went on to attribute to him the practice of decorating the fir tree. Although this claim has no historical merit, it reflects the memory that Luther was devoted to the day.

Other Protestants, however, were strongly opposed to Christmas. For many, keeping holy days represented residual "papist" tendencies since their dates had been prescribed by tradition and Church authorities, not Scripture. Moreover, there were concerns that Christmas had connections to pagan festivals. In the Middle Ages, certain features of the Roman festival of Saturnalia appear to have been continued at Christmas in highly inappropriate ways. For example, whereas masters served their slaves at table during Saturnalia in ancient Rome, the practice of a "boy bishop" was adopted in certain Christian cities. This would go as far as putting the bishop's garments on a boy and allowing him to lead certain activities (though not Masses) in churches.[8] The practice could easily slide into the realm of the sacrilegious.

The battle over Christmas was sharp in Protestant England, where Puritans made opposition to Christmas a central political issue. In 1647, the English Parliament legally abolished

---

8   Nicholas Orme, *Medieval Children* (New Haven, CT: Yale University Press, 2003), 188.

holy days, including Christmas. Those who ignored the edict and hung Christmas decorations were arrested. The celebration of Christmas was viewed through a political lens—those who did so were suspected of promoting a "papist" agenda. The Puritans who traveled to America shared these sentiments. Colonists in Plymouth and Massachusetts outlawed Christmas beginning in 1659, though the penalties were less strict than in England.

For New Englanders, Christmas was feared for reasons beyond theological objections. In the 1600s, it had become associated with "misrule" and civic disorder. Of particular concern was the way "wassailing" had evolved. Originally, the term referred to well-wishing. On its face, "wassailing" meant going from house to house, wishing others well. Over time, however, it had taken a dark turn.[9] Drunk revelers expected to be given something—money, drink, etc.—before moving on to another house. This came with implicit (and explicit) threats. As one popular wassailing song put it:

> We have come here to claim our right....
> If you don't open up your door,
> We will lay you flat upon the floor.

In other words, wassailing started to look something like extortion. Reports of it involved stories of home invasion, assault, and other crimes. All of this, sadly, became associated with Christmas.

In the end, however, the Puritans' opposition to Christmas could not endure. Although their efforts did lead to more subdued expressions of holiday cheer, they were unable to overcome its popularity. In England, Christmas was eventually

---

9   On this period, see Stephen Nissenbaum, *The Battle for Christmas: A Social and Cultural History of Our Most Cherished Holiday* (New York: Vantage, 1997), 5–11.

reinstated. Likewise, laws prohibiting the celebration of Christmas in the North American colonies were eventually overturned.

The Resurgence of Christmas

Still, the extent to which Christmas was observed varied from place to place. Many Christian churches kept their doors shut on Christmas Day. Some influential Americans began to be concerned about this. One of them was the prominent New Yorker John Pintard (1759–1844). Pintard was fond of holidays and believed a winter celebration was needed in American society. He observed Christmas, but only as a private, religious affair. Yet as the founding member of the New York Historical Society, he frequently expressed his desire to bring back old customs, including those he associated with Christmas. His desires were shared by one of his influential friends: Washington Irving (1783–1859).

Irving was the first American author to write books that went on to become best sellers in England. Like others in his circles, he was worried about the growing gap between rich and poor in America. With John Pintard, he thought that tapping into old traditions might help address the problem.

In 1819, he published a book called *The Sketch Book of Geoffrey Crayon, Gent*, which included two of his best-known stories, "Rip Van Winkle" and "The Legend of Sleepy Hollow." Five of the book's chapters, however, focused on Christmas. While his presentation included religious elements—for example, his characters recognize the date as marking "our Savior's birth" and even attend church services—special emphasis was given to the notion of the family Christmas meal in the home, which was depicted as an exceptionally joyful event. Irving remembered an older English tradition in which the wealthy would invite the poor into their homes on Christmas Day. This practice was fading in England, but Irving believed it could help bridge the gap between the rich and poor. On one level, he was effective: his stories helped remove Protestant embarrassment over celebrating Christmas. Nevertheless, his work did little to ignite deeper concerns for the poor.

Charles Dickens was influenced by Irving's work, but found a way to succeed where Irving had failed. In his landmark work, *A Christmas Carol*, Dickens gave names and faces to the less fortunate. In Bob Cratchit and his sickly son Tiny Tim, he humanized the weak and downtrodden. This was not a difficult task for Dickens. He knew well what the plight of the poor involved. Scholars have shown that *A Christmas Carol* reflects memories of his own childhood. Bob Cratchit is Scrooge's clerk—just as Dickens' own father had worked as a clerk. When Scrooge dismisses those collecting money for the poor, he callously insists that the workhouses and debtors' prisons "cost enough: and those who are badly off must go there." What readers did not know until he died was that Dickens' own father had been sent to prison because of debt. The Cratchits' home was a four-room flat located in Camden town—exactly like the place Dickens knew from his childhood. Dickens was able to personalize the experience of those in poverty because he had lived it himself.

Scrooge's heartless rhetoric may seem overblown at times. Yet it was not far off from the kinds of cruel things Dickens would have heard people in his day say about the poor. At one point, Scrooge insists that if the poor would rather die than go to prison, "they had better do it, and decrease the surplus population." As others have noted, Dickens here has Scrooge express a sentiment infamously articulated by Robert Malthus (1766–1834). In Malthus' work warning about the problem of overpopulation, he disturbingly argues that since the world's resources cannot sustain its peoples, it would be best for the poor and sickly to meet a premature death.[10]

Whereas Irving had presented a vision of "Christmas past," Dickens showed what it could be in the present. And while its primary focus was not the story of Christ's birth, it was also not a purely secular vision of the season. Scrooge is introduced as a "covetous old sinner" in need of salvation. But redemption cannot merely be about a personal transformation; it must include good works toward one's neighbor.

One especially poignant scene is worth highlighting. Tiny Tim tells his mother that he hopes people see him in church because

> it might be pleasant for them to remember upon Christmas day, [the one] who made lame beggars walk and blind men see.

The scene implicitly draws on Jesus' teaching. As he says in the Gospel of Matthew, caring for the poor is not simply an act of charity; it is to recognize that Christ is to be found in "the least of these my brothers" (Matthew 25:40). For Dickens, showing kindness to the poor was more than social work; it was about learning to recognize Christ in "the least of these." To renounce Christ's calling to recognize him in the poor was to be like Scrooge—a name evocative of Puritan stock. Christmas was the ideal time to show generosity to the poor. Who could protest?

Dickens successfully threaded the needle—he explained why Christmas was needed in Protestant Christianity. Still, there was one last vestige of "popery" that New Yorkers like John Pintard and Washington Irving wanted to bring back: a

---

10   See Carlo DeVito, *Inventing Scrooge: The Incredible True Story behind Dickens' Legendary "A Christmas Carol"* (Kennebunkport, ME: Cider Mills Press, 2014), 71–73.

patron saint. We bring this book to a close, then, with a discussion of how Saint Nicholas was transformed into Santa Claus.

How Saint Nicholas Became Santa Claus

For some Christians, Santa Claus is a problem. He represents the so-called "secular Christmas," which undermines the true meaning of the season. The reality, however, is that he has his roots in a saint from the early Church. How did Saint Nicholas become Santa Claus, and how did Nicholas become the "patron saint" of Christmas? The story serves as a fitting way to end our discussion of Christmas.

Saint Nicholas of Myra

While many have doubted his historical existence, more recent scholarship is showing that there is good reason to believe Saint Nicholas was a real person.[11] The earliest written accounts of his life—at least, the ones that still exist—were written hundreds of years after his death and use a great deal of poetic license. It is also evident that writers confused him with another person, Nicholas of Sion, who was born some two hundred years after the Nicholas who became known as Santa Claus. Here we can briefly state what historians can say with confidence.

In around A.D. 260, Nicholas was born in Patara, a city located in what is now the nation of Turkey. He went on to be ordained a priest. Eventually, he was made bishop of Myra, an

---

11   For a serious study, see Adam C. English, *The Saint Who Would Be Santa Claus: The True Life and Trials of Nicholas of Myra* (Waco, TX: Baylor University Press, 2012).

important seaport on the Mediterranean, also located in what is now modern-day Turkey.

We do not know much more for certain about Nicholas' ministry. Many believe he attended the Council of Nicaea in the year 325, though the evidence for this is uncertain. Many have heard that Nicholas struck the heretic Arius during the council's proceedings. There is no reliable evidence to support this. The source that first reports the episode dates to more than a thousand years after Nicholas' death. It strains credulity to think that earlier writers knew of it but failed to mention it. The claim that they passed over it in silence out of embarrassment is not believable; the story was told to emphasize Nicholas' orthodoxy. Despite the lack of reliable evidence, however, the story continues to be shared as a historical fact.

The Spread of Saint Nicholas' Reputation as a Gift-Giver

One of the most famous stories told about Nicholas is found in the earliest extant account of his life, written by Michael the Archimandrite in the 700s. As a young man, we learn, Nicholas' parents had died. They were of noble birth and had left Nicholas a great amount of wealth. Nicholas, however, is aware of Scripture's warnings about the dangers of riches. He therefore lives simply and looks for ways to help others with his money. He soon finds an important opportunity to do so.

Nicholas has a neighbor who is a virtuous man. The man's goodness angers Satan, "who always has a grudge against those who prefer to live a life in accord with God."[12] The

---

12 Michael the Archimandrite, "The Life of St. Nicholas the Wonderworker," trans. John Quinn, St. Nicholas Center (website), 2008, https://www.stnicholascenter.org/who-is-st-nicholas/stories -legends/classic-sources/michael-the-archimandrite.

devil therefore seeks a way to bring the man to spiritual ruin. Through his diabolical machinations, the devil orchestrates a series of events that causes the man to become destitute. He now has two problems. First, because he is unable to pay their dowries, he is unable to marry off his three beautiful daughters. Second, he is unable to feed himself and his family. Facing starvation, the man is finally driven to his breaking point. He begins to consider committing a grave sin; he thinks about selling his daughters into a life of prostitution.

When Nicholas learns of the situation, he resolves to use his own inheritance to rescue the man from sin and to save his daughters from a life of slavery. During the night, Nicholas sneaks over to his neighbor's house and throws a bag containing gold coins through his window. Upon realizing what someone has done for him, the neighbor immediately arranges the marriage of his first daughter. Nicholas tosses another bag of gold into the man's house the next night. Again, the man acts and finds a husband for his second daughter. He then asks the Lord to help him discover the identity of his mysterious benefactor. The following night, the man stays up, waiting to see if his anonymous patron will return. When Nicholas throws a third bag into his home, the father races outside and chases him down. Recognizing Nicholas, the man falls at the saint's feet, thanking him and praising God for working through the saint. Nicholas instructs the man not to reveal his generosity to others.

Later retellings of Nicholas' act of kindness would include familiar details. For example, in one account, the bags of money thrown into the house by Nicholas land in the girls' shoes. Another relates that before Nicholas had visited the house, the girls had hung their wet stockings by the fireplace to dry them. When Nicholas arrives, the windows are closed. Because of this, he throws the bags down the chimney. As you might expect, they land in the girls' stockings.

Since Myra was a port town, Saint Nicholas' reputation spread quickly. Sailors came to depend on his intercession. Before his time, the name *Nikolaos* is practically unknown. After the 300s, it (and derivations of it) is well-attested. It seems many were inspired to name their children after the great saint of Myra. By the end of the Middle Ages, Nicholas was known throughout Christendom. His feast day came to be celebrated on December 6.

Moreover, his example of generosity inspired the practice of giving gifts on his feast day.[13] In the 1100s, French nuns, taking Nicholas as their model, began leaving presents for poor children at their homes on December 6, signing them with the saint's name. Dutch and German parents began to leave treats for their little ones in their shoes or stockings. Saint Nicholas—and later "Santa Claus"—became a great cover for those who wished to give in the way mandated by Christ: "But when you give alms, do not let your left hand know what your right hand is doing, *that your alms may be in secret*: and *your Father who sees in secret shall repay you*" (Matthew 6:3–4).

Santa Claus Is Coming to Town

With the Protestant Reformation, however, the practice of honoring saints like Nicholas was deemed inappropriate in non-Catholic countries. Even though the book of Revelation contains a vision of those in heaven offering to God the prayers of those on earth (Revelation 5:8), asking saints in heaven to intercede on behalf of those on earth was viewed as theologically incorrect. How then did Nicholas become "Santa Claus"?

---

13 For what follows, see Adam C. English, "St. Nicholas to Santa Claus," in Larsen, *Oxford Handbook of Christmas*, 253–54.

Once again, enter influential New Yorker John Pintard. Looking for a way to refocus holiday celebrations on charity and kindness instead of raucous partying, Pintard promoted Saint Nicholas at the 1810 banquet of the New York Historical Society, which took place on December 6. The night opened with a toast to "Sancte Claus." After this event, Nicholas' profile in New York began to rise. Just two weeks after the gala, a poem appeared in a New York paper about the saint. It was presented as a child's description of him. In it he is called "Sancte Claus" and is identified as one who rewards good children. One line reads, "From naughty behavior we'll always refrain / In hopes that you'll come and reward us again."

When Pintard's friend Washington Irving wrote his wildly popular fictional history of New York, known as *Diedrich Knickerbocker's History of New York* (1809), he turned Nicholas into the city's patron saint. In Irving's fanciful account of the founding of New York, Dutch settlers arrive on a ship bearing the saint's image. In the revised edition of the book published in 1812, the saint appears to a Dutch man named Van Cortland in a dream:

> And when St. Nicholas had smoked his pipe, he twisted it in his hat-band, and laying his finger beside his nose, gave the astonished Van Cortland a very significant look, then, mounting his wagon, he returned over the tree-tops and disappeared.

One can see here elements that would become central to depictions of Santa Claus.

In 1823, *The Sentinel*, a paper in Troy, New York, published a poem it had received from an anonymous author. Although it was originally titled "An Account of a Visit from Saint Nicholas," it is more commonly known today by its first line: " 'Twas the Night Before Christmas." The piece presented a picture of Saint Nicholas that included elements taken up from other writers such as Irving. It came to be attributed to Clement Clarke Moore (1779–1863), a wealthy New York patrician who was a Bible scholar and a professor of Hebrew. Moore was also friends with Pintard and Irving. After years of being its rumored author, Moore finally acknowledged that he had written it. However, some now believe it was penned by a Dutch American named Henry Livingston (1748–1828), who published other anonymous pieces that resemble " 'Twas the Night Before Christmas."[14] Livingston died before Moore accepted authorship of it. Regardless of who wrote it, the account played a key role in the cultural transformation of Christmas in the West, beginning in America.

Irving's writings had helped clear the way for reimagining how Christmas festivities should be conceived. Instead of primarily being celebrated in "the streets and pubs," Christmas was now becoming associated with "hearth and home."[15] The poem about Saint Nicholas' visit on Christmas Eve cemented the sense that the day was best observed by basking in the warmth of the fireplace and in the company of joyful innocence rather than with rowdy revelers.

Of course, a key feature of the poem was that Nicholas brought presents not on December 6 but on Christmas Eve. This furthered another shift. Whereas New Year's Day had previously been seen as the time for gift-giving, Christmas would now assume that position. For those who wished to give in secret like Christ mandated, Santa Claus offered much. As one historian sums up the attitude, "To give in a Christian manner, is to be a secret Santa."[16] Not surprisingly, it was *churches* and not stores where Santa Claus appearances first

---

14 See ibid., 258–59.

15 Ibid., 258.

16 Timothy Larsen, "Nineteenth Century," in Larsen, *Oxford Handbook of Christmas*, 43. The rest of this paragraph is indebted to his research.

became popular. In fact, to find a Santa costume one had to order it through a religious supplies company.

Of course, the poem therefore was also especially appealing to retailers. Particularly helpful to them was this line about Saint Nicholas: "A bundle of toys he had flung on his back / And he looked like a peddler just opening his pack." Peddlers could not be so bad if Saint Nicholas himself could be counted among them.

As for his name, that had been evolving for some time. In 1773, the *Rivington's Gazeteer* mentioned December 6 as the day of Nicholas "otherwise called St. a Claus." In Germany, he had been known as "Kris Kringle," which was derived from *Christkindl*, the "Christ child." The tradition is attributed to Martin Luther, who is said to have encouraged the idea that Christ himself came bearing gifts on Christmas. Over time, the gift-bearer became a sort of angel or gnome. In the Netherlands, Nicholas became known as *Sinterklaas*. In England, he was called "Father Christmas."

It was advertisers who helped standardize the name "Santa Claus" as well as his appearance. By the end of the 1800s, men in Santa Claus outfits were ringing bells on sidewalks and drawing customers into stores. Most famous, perhaps, is Coca-Cola's use of Santa Claus. Beginning in 1931, the company's marketing campaigns famously featured now-iconic depictions of Santa drawn by Haddon Sundblom.

Gathered around the Tree with a Saint

The poem about Saint Nicholas' late-night visit never mentions a Christmas tree, yet one can easily see how their popularity helped further reinforce the notion that the season is best celebrated at home. Like Saint Nicholas, the tree also has religious origins. Contrary to popular opinion, historian David

Bertaina shows that the practice of decorating trees for Christmas probably does not have its origins in pagan practices.[17] Rather, it seems more likely that the custom evolved out of medieval plays that dramatized Bible stories. In these performances, a tree was often used to symbolize both the Fall of humanity in the garden and the redemption of the world that takes place through Christ's Cross, understood to be the true "tree of life." It appears that the guilds who sponsored these plays did so to raise their profile. It seems they used decorated trees for promotion. By the 1400s, the symbolism was further developed; trees were decorated with apples (a symbol of the Fall) and wafers (to signify the Eucharist).

We have evidence that people began to use trees for home decoration at Christmas in sixteenth-century Germany, where they also started to be used in churches. The English royal family first adopted the Christmas tree in the 1800s. Its use in American homes seems to have developed shortly thereafter. As Christmas became a feast especially localized in the home, the Christmas tree only grew in popularity.

For some believers, like the Protestant Puritans of old, features of the modern-day Christmas like Santa Claus and the Christmas tree are necessarily a distraction from the central mystery the season is meant to honor: the birth of Christ the Lord. Ironically, it was largely Protestants like John Pintard and Washington Irving who helped turn the early Christian bishop into a prominent part of the West's Christmas customs as we know them today. These men were responsible for helping a Protestant culture embrace a feast that many believed was contrary to biblical Christianity. The appeal of the good Saint Nicholas was too much for anti-Catholic tendencies to withstand. Without a concrete example of goodness, the

---

17 See David Bertaina, "Trees and Decorations," in Larsen, *Oxford Handbook of Christmas*, 265–76.

way to celebrate Christmas properly remained dangerously abstract.

Yet the mystery of Christ's nativity is, as we have seen, ultimately about the world's redemption; Joseph is instructed to name the child Jesus because "he shall save his people from their sins" (Matthew 1:21). Salvation, as I explain in my previous book *Salvation: What Every Catholic Should Know*, is more than simply about God delivering humanity from hell. Rather, it is about becoming "conformed to the image of his Son" (Romans 8:29). In the New Testament, humanity is redeemed by being united to Christ and being transformed in the process. Saint Nicholas represents what the Savior was born to accomplish in the fallen children of Adam.

In the story of the saint's famous act of charity, the man saved by Nicholas' generosity says the following: "If our common Master, Christ, hadn't stirred your goodness, we would have long ago destroyed our own lives by a shameful and destructive livelihood." At Christmas, we celebrate the one who was born to die on a tree so that goodness could become a reality in us. We are invited to the greatest homecoming of all—we are united to become part of the family of God in the Divine Son, gathered "round yon Virgin," Joseph, and the other saints. The memory of Nicholas reminds us that becoming like Christ is possible. Before we gather around the Christmas tree, let us gather also to Christ in the Church's celebration where, with saints like Nicholas, we pray to learn to give ourselves away by the gift of his grace, singing his praise in the familiar hymns we have all known: "O Come, Let Us Adore Him / Christ the Lord."

Acknowledgments

I would like to offer a brief word of thanks to those people who were especially involved in helping me as I wrote this book. Of course, all the book's deficiencies are to be attributed to me alone. Nonetheless, so many people made this book not only possible but also much better than it would have otherwise been. First, I thank John Cavadini for his beautiful Foreword.

Second, I express my gratitude to everyone at the Augustine Institute Graduate School who have enabled me to pursue this project. I owe special thanks to President Tim Gray for supporting this project and for making some suggestions that improved the presentation of the material here. I also must mention Christopher Blum. Without his support as dean, this book would never have been possible. In addition, I am extremely grateful to my colleagues on the faculty for numerous conversations that shaped this book's contents in important ways: Mark Giszczak, Ben Akers, Elizabeth Klein, Scott Heffelfinger, and Lucas Pollice. I am thankful to Jim Prothro and Daniel Moloney, who also read various chapters and offered extremely insightful feedback and editorial suggestions.

In addition, I must thank Mark Middendorf for his incredible support and for his vital help in the process of naming the book. I also thank Joseph Pearce for his fine work as editor. In addition, I am grateful to Kris Gray, Julie Musselman, Dennis McCarthy, and Susan Wood for all their help on this project. Finally, to Ben Dybas I am grateful for the beautiful cover.

I am especially indebted to three dear friends who pored over the entire manuscript, offering invaluable suggestions: Brant Pitre, John Kincaid, and John Sehorn. Their help profoundly improved this book. I am especially grateful to Brant for offering his help at an especially inconvenient time.

I must also express gratitude to Father Andrew Younan, Thomas Harmon, and Matthew Peterson for being a sounding board and for helping me settle on the book's title.

I also wish to thank Father Joseph Fessio and Mark Brumley for reading the manuscript carefully and offering observations that strengthened it. In addition, I thank others at Ignatius Press who helped work on this book.

Likewise, I thank my siblings—Noree, Tracee, Julia, Marita, and Georgie—for giving me feedback on various aspects of the book. The same goes to my uncle Father Peter Irving, and my aunts Rita Irving and Marty Irving. Of course, my love of Christmas is especially due to a lifetime of celebrating it with them.

I am profoundly grateful to my children—Michael, Matthew, Molly, Thomas, Susanna, and Simon—for all their patience as I worked on this project, which involved many late nights at the office.

Above all, I have to thank my wife, Kimberly, for supporting this book. She made innumerable sacrifices that made it possible for me to complete this project. Among other things, she carefully read every chapter, offering vital advice. Her faithfulness speaks more eloquently of the truth of the Christmas mystery of the Incarnation than I could ever articulate in a book.

Finally, I dedicate this book to my parents, Patrick and Theresa Barber, who always taught me how to celebrate Christmas in such a way that its true meaning in Christ was always of foremost importance. In Christ, I am always with them and home for Christmas.

SUBJECT INDEX

Africanus, Julius, 158, 159, 161, 162

Allison, Dale C., Jr., 74n3, 113n2, 114n5, 122n18, 122n19, 124, 124n25, 125n26, 128n30, 139, 139n12

Aquinas, 77, 77n8

Augustine of Canterbury, 173

Augustine of Hippo, 48, 49, 49n6, 73, 73n1, 77, 77n7, 107, 107n3, 164, 164n32, 172, 172n5, 173

Aune, David, 141, 141n18, 142

Baden, Joel S., 61n11

Bailey, Kenneth, 92n6, 94, 94n14

Barber, Michael P., xiv, xvi, 19n6, 19n7, 31n5, 136n5

Bede the Venerable, 119, 173

Bergsma, John S., 18n5

Bertaina, David, 186–87, 187n17

Bond, Helen K., 141n17

Brown, Raymond, 60, 60n10, 61, 91n4, 106n2, 115n6, 117n10, 120n13, 123n22, 127n28

Burridge, Richard, 141n16

Carlson, Stephen, 89n3

Christmas lights, 89

Christmas trees, 166, 167, 186, 187, 188

Chrysostom, 2, 2n1, 77, 77n7, 96, 96n16, 98, 121, 122, 122n18, 150, 150n7, 151

Church of the Nativity (in Bethlehem), 94, 114, 115

Clement of Alexandria, 126, 126n27, 147, 147n1, 148, 163n31

Collins, Adela Yarbro, 16n3

Collins, John, 11n1, 16n3, 123, 123n21

Cyril of Alexandria, 95, 96n15

Davies, W. D., 74n3, 113n2, 124, 124n25, 125n26

Day, John, 153n12

de la Potterie, Ignace, 77, 77n8

DeVito, Carlo, 179n10

Dickens, Charles, 1, 2, 4, 5, 178, 179

Eckhardt, Benedikt, 25n2

Egeria, 148, 148n3

Ehrman, Bart, 60n9, 134, 135n4

English, Adam C., 180n11, 183n13, 185n14, 185n15

Ephrem, 82, 82n11

Epiphanius, 148, 148n4

Epiphany, 168, 170, 171

Eusebius, 93, 93n10, 93n12, 124, 124n24

Evans, Craig A., 102n1

Farkasfalvy, Denis, 48, 48n4

Fiensy, David A., 91n5

Filas, Francis L., 82n11

Fitzmyer, Joseph A., 140n13

Foreman, Benjamin A., 89n3
Francis of Assisi, 88
frankincense, 111, 112, 116, 117,
    118, 125, 126
Friedlieb, Josef Heinrich, 151,
    151n8

Gregory the Great, 97, 97n19,
    107, 108, 108n4, 121,
    121n17, 173, 173n6
Gurtner, Daniel M., 25n2

Hamm, Dennis, 26n4
Handel, George Frideric, 15
Hays, Richard, 34, 34n9
Hijmans, Steven, 156n17
Hippolytus, 156n18, 159,
    159n25, 160, 160n28

Incarnation, xi, xv, xvi, 33, 145
integral age view, 157
Irenaeus, 69, 69n21, 70, 126,
    126n27, 129
Irving, Washington, 177, 178,
    179, 184, 185, 187

Jacob of Voragine, 170, 170n3
Jerome, 44, 45, 65, 65n20, 77,
    77n9, 79, 92, 92n7, 93,
    93n12, 96, 97n18, 123n22,
    164, 164n33
Jesse Tree, 14
Jewish marriage practices
    (ancient), 75–76
Joseph's age at the time of Jesus'
    birth, 80–81
Josephus, 25n3, 62n15, 121,
    121n16, 136, 137, 137n6,
    137n7
Justin Martyr, 53n1, 74, 74n2,
    77, 77n6, 93, 93n8, 115,
    115n7, 154, 154n14

Keener, Craig S., 112n1, 139n11
Kelly, Joseph F., 89, 89n2, 98n20,
    119n11
Kincaid, John A., 19n7, 31n5

Landry, David T., 59, 59n7
Larsen, Timothy, 2n2, 128n29,
    174n7, 183n13, 185n16,
    187n17
Las Posadas, 89
Last Supper, 94–95
Leo the Great, 48, 48n5, 108,
    108n5, 130, 130n31, 164,
    165n34, 165n35
Levine, Amy-Jill, 41n2
Levine, Baruch, 61n14
Luther, Martin, 85, 175, 186
Luz, Ulrich, 125n26

Malthus, Robert, 178–79
Marcus, Joel, 64n19
Mary as the New Eve, 69–70
McDowell, Sean, 170n2
Meier, John P., 55, 55n4, 137n6,
    137n8
Michael the Archimandrite, 181,
    181n12
Midnight Mass, origins of, 97–98
Milgrom, Jacob, 61, 61n14
Moss, Candida R., 61n11
Mosshammer, Alden A., 158n23,
    160n29
myrrh, 111, 116, 120, 125, 126

Newman, John Henry, 154, 154n15
New Year's celebration, 3, 172,
    185
Nicholas, Saint, 6, 167, 180–88
Nissenbaum, Stephen, 176n9
Nolland, John, 60n8
Nothaft, C. Philipp E., 159n24
Novenson, Matthew V., 11n1

Origen, xi, xin1, xin2, xin3, xii, xiin4, xiii, xiiin5, xiv, xivn6, xivn7, xv, xvn8, xvn9, xvn10, xvi, xviin14, xviin15, 45, 45n3, 93, 93n9, 96, 96n17, 115, 116, 116n8, 116n9, 117, 123n22, 126, 126n27, 130, 134n1, 163n31

Perry, Joe, 174n7
Philo, 31, 61n13, 62n15, 113n3, 124, 124n23
Pintard, John, 177, 179, 184, 185, 187
Pitre, Brant, 19n7, 31n5, 59, 59n6, 61, 61n12, 158n21
Pleše, Zlatko, 60n9
Prothro, James, 62n18

Rahner, Karl, 77, 77n8
Roll, Susan K., 148n2, 165n35
Rowe, C. Kavin, 31, 31n6, 32, 32n7
Ryan, Jordan J., 94n13

S., Acharya (D. M. Murdoch), 134, 134n2, 134n3, 135
Sanders, E. P., 25n3
Santa Claus, 6, 166, 167, 180, 183, 184, 185, 186, 187

Saturnalia, 155, 155n16, 172, 175
Saulnier, Stéphane, 152n11
Schmidt, Thomas C., 156n18, 159n25, 160n27, 161n30
Seitz, Christopher, 17n4
Sextus Empiricus, 141n14, 141n15
Sol Invictus, 155–156, 165
Sri, Edward, 57n5
Staples, Jason, 33, 33n8
Stephen (martyr), 45, 169, 170
Struckenbruck, Loren T., 25n2
Suetonius, 120, 121n15, 137, 137n9

Tacitus, 137
Tertullian, 115, 115n7, 154n13, 160, 160n26, 161, 169, 170n1
Thompson, Augustine, 88n1
Treggiari, Susan, 154n13

Virgil, 120, 120n14

Weksler-Bdolah, Schlomit, 93n11
Williams, D. H., 128n29, 130n31
Witakoswki, Witold, 119n12
Wolff, Hans Walter, 54n2

"YHWH," 31
Yule, 172, 174

SCRIPTURE INDEX

Genesis

1:14	162
3:20	70
3:24	107
4:1	69
13:8	63
24:16	56
24:43	56
26:26	116
26:28	117
35:21	54n3
37:5–11	81

Exodus

1:15–21	128
2:1–10	128
2:15	128
3:1	100
12:6	158
13:2	66
20:7	31
20:8–10	18
22:18	113
23:26	157
25:22	41
26:33–35	41
28:41	12
29:38–42	26
30:4–8	126
30:30	12
40:13, 15	12
40:34	106
40:35	41

Leviticus

12:8	74
16:30	19
16:32	12
23:36	169
24:7	126
25:1–7	18
25:8–55	18
25:9	19
25:25–34	19
25:39–55	19

Numbers

3:12	66
6:3	28
6:5	28
7:9	42
22:31	26
24:17–19	123
24:18	124
28:3–8	26
30:13	61

Deuteronomy

13:10	113
18:10	113
20:7	75
22:13–29	77
28:1–14	9
28:25, 49–51	9
28:30	75
28:64	9
32:17	153

Judges

13:4–5	29
14:15	75

1 Samuel

1:11	29
16:11	101
16:13	12
24:10	12
24:14	114
26:9, 11	12

2 Samuel

5:2	87
6:2	41, 43
6:6–7	42
6:11	42
6:23	65
7:1	9
7:8	101
7:9, 13, 14, 16	39
7:12–14	12
7:12–16	52

1 Kings

2:19–20	57
4:7	58
4:20–21	9
4:29–34	14
19:16	12

2 Kings

4:1–7	19
6:16	105

2 Kings (*continued*)
6:17   105
10:13   57
18:7   16

1 Chronicles
24:4   25–26
29:20   125

Ezra
9:5–7   28
9:8–9   10

Nehemiah
9:36   10

Judith
9:1–14   28

Job
36:26   153

Psalms
2:2   15, 127
2:7   40
2:7–9   15
71:13–14   118
72:10–11   118
78:49   26
102:25   153

Proverbs
1:1   114

Wisdom of Solomon
7:4   88
18:14–15   97

Sirach
38:27   74
48:10   29

Isaiah
1:3   92
6:3   106
7:14   16, 33, 52,
              54–56
7:14, 16   52
8:8   53
9:6   33
9:6–7   16, 106
9:7   16
11:1–2, 4   13–14
11:6   14
14:12   123
37:36   26
40:1–3   10
40:3   31
40:9   11
53:3   109
53:12   109
60:1–14   126
60:6, 10–11   117
61:1   12
61:1–2   20
65:17   66
66:22   15

Jeremiah
6:20   126
29:2   57
31:15   144

Ezekiel
16:4   89
32:7   123

Daniel
1:7   119
2:2, 10   113n3
2:10, 27   113
9:5, 11   17
9:21   27

9:24   18, 19, 20
9:25   20
10:7   26

Micah
5:2   87
5:2–3   54, 54n3
7:6   129

Habakkuk
2:20   133

Malachi
4:2   162
4:5–6   29

2 Maccabees
3:22–34   27
7:23   67

Matthew
1:1–17   72
1:18   77
1:18–19   75
1:19   80
1:20   77, 78
1:20–21   81
1:21   119, 188
1:22–23   52
1:23   117, 125
1:25   65, 75
2:1   114
2:1–2   112
2:2   74, 126
2:3–6   54
2:4   127
2:4–6   87
2:8–9, 11   128
2:9   121
2:10–11   117
2:11   116, 118, 125

2:12   114, 130
2:13   79
2:13–15   128
2:16   74, 128, 130,
              169
2:17–18   144
2:19–21   128
2:20   79
3:17   xii
5:19   79
5:31   76
6:3–4   183
6:12   19
7:21   33, 55
9:9–13   115
10:1–7   139
10:34–35   129
12:46   80
13:38   70
13:54–55   73
13:55   72
13:55–56   63
16:24   131
19:3, 7–9   76
19:28   58, 67
20:28   119
22:30   68
25:11   55
25:40   179
26:3   127
26:17–19   158
26:38   xii
26:57   127
27:11   127
27:29   127
27:29, 37   114
27:37   127
27:42   114
27:62   127
28:19   55, 114
28:20   65

Mark
1:11   xii
3:31   80
6:3   40, 63, 64
6:7–13   139
12:25   68
14:12–16   158
14:34   xii
15:7   103
15:23   126
15:40–41   63
15:42   158

Luke
1:1–4   137–38
1:5   151
1:5–7   24
1:6   25
1:8–10   25
1:10   26
1:11   26, 46
1:12   46, 101
1:13   28, 44, 46
1:13–15   27
1:15   33
1:15–17   28
1:16–17   30, 33–34
1:17   29
1:18   30, 46, 59, 80
1:19   27
1:20   30, 46
1:24, 26, 36   149,
              150
1:26   46
1:27   80
1:28   44, 47, 104
1:30   44, 46
1:31   46
1:31–33   39
1:32   39, 40
1:33   39

1:34   46, 58
1:35   40
1:37   35
1:38   46
1:39–45   47
1:42–43   32
1:43   32, 92
1:45   32
1:46, 48   47
1:48, 51–53   100
1:57–63   81
1:57–64   30
1:62–63   80
1:68–79   30
1:78   162
2:1   101
2:1–6   87
2:6   90
2:7   66, 88, 89–90,
              91, 92
2:7, 12, 16   92
2:8   97, 100, 149
2:9   106
2:10   xiv, 101
2:10–12   102
2:11   104, 106
2:12   40, 128
2:13   99
2:13–14   104, 106
2:14   106
2:18   90
2:21   169
2:24   74, 171
2:26–35   130
2:35   130
3:1   158
3:3   30
3:22   xii, 29, 107
3:23–38   69
4:9–11   105
4:21   21

Luke (*continued*)

6:46	33
8:19	80
9:1–2	139
10:34	90
11:27	40
14:22	90
15:10	104
19:6	104
20:34–35	67
22:7–13	158
22:10–13	95
22:11	90
22:19	95
22:30	58
22:37	109
23:54	158

John

1:1	33
1:4–5, 7–9	162
1:14	33
1:34	xii
1:49	114
2:1–11	168
2:3	57
2:12	80
3:16	33, 48
6:51	97
8:12	162
9:5	162
13:1–2	158
19:25	64, 65
19:31	158

19:35	138
19:39	126
21:24	138

Acts

6:8	45
7:54–60	169
8:9–11	113
13:4–8	113
13:10	114
23:6	11

Romans

3:23–24	44
5:14	70
8:29	188

1 Corinthians

1:25	xv
7:17	68
7:31	68
7:33	68
7:34	68
7:38	68
9:14	139
11:2	140
11:23	140
11:23–24	140
15:3	140
15:45	70

2 Corinthians

4:7	xvii
5:17	69

Galatians

2:9	138

Ephesians

1:6	47
2:14	108

Philippians

2:7	xii, xiii

Colossians

1:15	xi
1:16	xi, xii
3:1	xv

Hebrews

9:3	41

James

5:16	109

1 Peter

4:13	109

2 Peter

1:16	143

Revelation

1:16	162
5:8	183
12:1	57